Landscapes of

WESTERN
PROVENCE
and Languedoc-Roussillon

a countryside guide

John and Pat Underwood

SUNFLOWER BOOKS

First published 2002
by Sunflower Books™
12 Kendrick Mews
London SW7 3HG, UK

ISBN 1-85691-194-2

Important note to the reader

We have tried to ensure that the descriptions and maps in this book are error-free at press date. The book will be updated, where necessary, whenever future printings permit. It will be very helpful for us to receive your comments (sent in care of the publishers, please) for the updating of future printings.

We also rely on those who use this book — especially walkers — to take along a good supply of common sense when they explore. Conditions can change fairly rapidly, and *storm damage or bulldozing may make a route unsafe at any time*. If the route is not as we outline it here, and your way ahead is not secure, return to the point of departure. *Never attempt to complete a tour or walk under hazardous conditions!* Please read carefully the Country code on page 7 and the notes on pages 55-57, as well as the introductory comments at the beginning of each tour and walk (regarding road conditions, equipment, grade, distances and time, etc). Explore *safely*, while at the same time respecting the beauty of the countryside.

Cover photograph: Pont du Gard (Car tours 4-7, Walk 7)
Page 1: traditional village sign, still seen in Hérault (Car tour 8)
Above: the Sphinx at Montpellier-le-Vieux (Walk 19)

Photographs: John Underwood
Maps: John Underwood
A CIP catalogue record for this book is available from the British Library.
Printed and bound in the UK by Brightsea Press, Exeter

10 9 8 7 6 5 4 3 2 1

❀ Contents

4 Landscapes of western Provence

Young cherry trees planted out south of Murs (Car tour 2), with the Lubéron rising through haze in the background. An example of the perfect harmony between man and nature that is the secret of the French countryside.

Preface

This two-volume *Landscapes of Provence* will plunge you into the most beautiful countryside between the Alps and the Pyrenees. Nature has prepared the canvas for these landscapes over millions of years, but man has added colour, form and texture. The straight bold strokes of lavender, vineyards, planes and poplars streak across plateaus; bridges and aqueducts arc gracefully over rivers; sturdy stone towers with whimsical wrought-iron bell-cages stipple the hilltops.

If the harmony between man and nature is the key to the beauty of this countryside, nowhere is it better conveyed than in the paintings of the Impressionists and Post-Impressionists so intimately associated with the South of France — Cézanne, Van Gogh, Monet. Almost everywhere you travel a masterpiece comes to life — an isolated farmhouse awash in fields of scarlet poppies, the limestone ribs of Ste-Victoire rising above a bib of emerald vineyards, stars burning out in a cobalt blue sky over the lamplit lanes of Arles.

This is a guide to the outdoors, written for those who prize the countryside as highly as a cathedral. We want to take you along the most beautiful roads by car and, when the opportunity presents itself, park, don walking boots, pick up the rucksack and *participate* in this landscape. France caters marvellously for all grades of walkers, but *precise* descriptions of tours and walks for motorists are rare. Most touring guides concentrate on history and architecture, while books for walkers outline the famous long-distance routes (the Grandes Randonnées). But these 'GR' footpaths are sometimes very demanding and, being linear, are in any case unsuitable for motorists.

Our aim has been to describe **car tours** running from the Italian border to the Pyrenees through *most* (certainly not all!) of the most beautiful scenery in the south of France. The **walks** chosen — from a vast network of possible routes — are those we feel offer the greatest sense of satisfaction for the effort involved, taking into account the high temperatures and humidity during much of the year. Most of the routes are circular.

The first volume of *Landscapes of Provence* travels from the Alps to Aix-en-Provence. This book will take you through western Provence and Languedoc-Roussillon to Canigou, sacred mountain of the Pyrenees. Use *Landscapes of the Pyrenees* to carry on to the Atlantic coast!

Bibliography

It must be stressed that this is a *countryside* guide, meant to be used in conjunction with a standard guide or guides covering the area. We find the Michelin guides indispensable, and always take along the following:

Michelin Red Guide: *always travel with the **latest** edition*. Not only is it useful for finding accommodation (and telephoning ahead), but the excellent plans are *essential* for finding your way round the cities.

Michelin Green Guides: Provence and **Pyrenees, Languedoc and Tarn Gorges** (both available in English).

Of the plethora of standard guides on the market, the **Cadogan Guide to the South of France** matches most closely the territory covered in the two volumes of *Landscapes of Provence;* its presentation and suggestions for places to stay should appeal to 'Landscapers'.

Many French **walking guides** are now available locally. Few tourist offices hand out free walk descriptions (as they did in the past); they prefer to sell you a book or map. If they *do* offer a free handout, it is likely to be virtually unreadable. Note that most French publications tend to describe walks *very briefly:* make sure that you can form a mental picture of the walk in advance — the climb, the distance, the terrain. Read carefully what we say on page 56 under 'Waymarking, grading, safety'.

MAPS

At the top of each **car tour** we refer to the appropriate **Michelin maps** (yellow series; scale 1:200,000). For this book you will need maps 80, 81, 83, 84 and 86 *or* the larger-format maps 240 (Languedoc/ Roussillon), 235 (Midi-Pyrénées) and 245 (Provence/Côte d'Azur); you may like to supplement these with the larger-scale map 114 (French Riviera/Var; scale 1:100,000).

For **walking** we hope that you will find the maps in the book sufficient. But if you plan to do a lot of walking in a given area, *do* buy the relevant **IGN 'Top 25' map**. These maps (scale 1:25,000), published by the Institut Géographique National (the French 'OS'), are widely available in shops, petrol stations and kiosks locally, or they may be purchased before you travel from your usual map supplier. For each walk in this book, the corresponding IGN map number is shown.

☀ Picnicking

Picnicking possibilities are limitless in Provence — especially if you follow the example of the locals and tour with a collapsible table and chairs (available at very low cost in the supermarkets). Picnic areas with tables are encountered on some of the tours; these are indicated in the touring notes and on the touring map with the symbol ⊼. All the walks in the book offer superb picnic settings, but on days when you are planning *only* to tour by car it is helpful to have some idea of where you might stop for an alfresco lunch. At the top of each car tour we suggest a few picnic spots, favourites of ours over the years. They are highlighted on the touring map, with a *P* printed in green. Where possible we have chosen places where there is something firm and dry to sit on.

A country code for walkers and motorists

Bear in mind that all land in the south of France is privately owned, whether by an individual or a district. All waymarked walks and other routes described in this book are permissive, *not* 'rights of way'. Behave responsibly, never forgetting the danger of forest fires.

- **Do not light fires** except at purpose-built barbecues. *Never park your car blocking a fire-fighting track!*
- **Do not frighten animals**. When driving, always stop the car until the livestock have moved off the road.
- **Walk quietly** through all farms, hamlets and villages, **leaving any gates just as you find them.**
- **Protect all wild and cultivated plants**. Don't pick wild flowers or uproot saplings. Obviously crops are someone's livelihood and should not be touched. **Never walk over cultivated land!**
- **Take all your litter away with you**.
- **Stay on the path**. Don't take short cuts on zigzag paths; this damages vegetation and hastens erosion, eventually destroying the main path.

Misty morning by the Rhône at Avignon (Car tour 4)

❀ Touring

The 12 car tours in this second volume of *Landscapes of Provence* take you west from Aix through Languedoc-Roussillon to the eastern Pyrenees. While a few important centres have been omitted for lack of space, we feel that the two books present a comprehensive overview of the most beautiful landscapes.

The touring notes are brief: they include little history or information readily available in other publications (see Bibliography, page 6). *We concentrate instead on route planning:* each tour has been devised to follow **the most beautiful roads** in the relevant region and to take you to the starting point of some delightful **walks**. (Further information about some of the places visited can be found in the notes for the walks.)

The large fold-out map is designed to give you a quick overview of the touring routes, walks and picnic places *in both volumes.* At the start of each tour we refer to the relevant Michelin touring map(s), which are so handy to use in conjunction with their *Red Guide.* **Important:** *Both driver and navigator should look over the* **latest Michelin Red Guide** *before entering or leaving any large city,* so that you have some idea of where you are heading and landmarks en route. It is *never* as simple as it looks on the touring maps, and *hours* can be wasted twirling in spaghetti loops on ring roads round cities like Aix or Nîmes!

The **touring bases** are, obviously, just *guidelines,* and the tours can be joined at any point en route (the major villages are shown at the top of each tour). Since some of the territory covered is well away from popular tourist

Early morning at Navacelles
(Car tour 8, Walk 18)

areas, we chose bases which offered not only hotels, but *our* essential requirements for making an early-morning start: a petrol station and a mini-market!

Because this is a *countryside* guide, the tours often bypass the villages en route, however beautiful or historically important. We do, however, use symbols to alert you to the cultural highlights (a **key to the symbols** used is on the touring map).

Some other points to keep in mind: **petrol stations** are often closed on Sundays and holidays in the remote areas covered by some of the tours. **Cyclists** do *not* travel in single file, nor is cycling confined to weekends. But on Sundays some roads will be closed off for cycle races: you will have to take a short *déviation*. **Déviations**, however, are *not* short when they involve roadworks. Especially in spring, long stretches of road will be closed, and you may have to go up to 50km out of your way! French **arrow signposting** is mystifying until you get used to it. Finally, remember that **Sundays and holidays** are a nightmare at the most popular 'sights'; monuments like the Pont du Gard or Les Baux should be avoided at all costs. Our tours have been planned not only to take you via the most beautiful roads, but to reach the three-star attractions before or after the crowds. If you follow our advice, but you *still* encounter crowds, we have to admit: we never visit Provence in July or August.

Tour 1: NATURE TAMED BY INDUSTRY

Aix-en-Provence • Rochers des Mées • Sisteron • St-Etienne-les-Orgues • Montagne de Lure • Banon • Simiane-la-Rotonde • Apt • Roussillon

255km/158mi; about 7h driving; Michelin map 84 (or larger-scale map 114) to begin, then map 81
Walks en route: 1, 2; *also Walks 35 and 36 in the companion volume (Eastern Provence)*
Because this is a very long tour, we use the motorway to start. If you can break the tour into two days, take the N96 from Aix, make a detour to Forcalquier and the Observatoire de Haute-Provence, then rejoin our tour at the Rochers des Mées. Sisteron would be a good place to break the tour. The road to the Signal de Lure is very narrow and winding and becomes vertiginous above tree-line;
on Sundays and in high season nervous drivers and passengers may prefer to turn back after Notre-Dame-de-Lure.

Picnic suggestions: The Lure mountain is climbed about half-way through the tour. At the chapel of **Notre-Dame-de-Lure** (⊼; photograph page 12) you will find shaded tables and benches, or you can sit on the chapel steps. At the end of the tour follow Short walk 2 (page 60), to picnic in **Roussillon's ocre quarries** (photograph page 61); there is ample shade and plenty of room to get away from other visitors.

The Durance rises near Briançon, a frothing Alpine stream. By the time it has raged through to the Mediterranean basin, the now-wide river runs sluggishly over its pebbly bed, tamed by the many dams and canals which today control its flow, watering the thirsty soil of Provence and powering many new industries. From the weird metallic beauty of the modern industrial landscape rising on the banks of this milky-turquoise river, we move on to a totally different 'industrial' landscape — the ocre quarries of Vaucluse.

Our journey west to the Pyrenees begins at **Aix-en-Provence** (described, with walk suggestions, in *Landscapes of eastern Provence*).

Head north from Aix on the A51 motorway.

You cross the **Canal EDF** (Electricité de France), one of the most important canals fed by the Durance. A sign tells announces your entry to the **Lubéron**, and the mountain is seen ahead, straddling the horizon. The motorway curves round to head east, with the Durance on the left, but the river isn't glimpsed until near

The approach to Sisteron

Pont-Mirabeau, where a picnic area (⊼) overlooks the pebbly river bed and desultory streams of turquoise water. The **Durance** is crossed (44km) just west of its confluence with the Verdon (its last major tributary); the small **Barrage de Cadarache** is on the right. Under 3km further on you are welcomed into the **Alpes-de-Haute-Provence**. On the west side of the river wide fields, with enormous gantries for irrigation, fill the space between the honey-coloured village of Ste-Tulle and the spread of Manosque. At the **Aire de Manosque** (⬛⊼) there

are some strange 'sculptures', characteristic of French motorway picnic areas — and a fine view over the wide river bed and frayed stream. One can easily imagine how destructive the river could be before it was harnessed. The motorway crosses the wide Canal EDF again, which in turn crosses the Durance on your right.

Leave the motorway at Exit 19, for FORCALQUIER, ORAISON. Then take the D4b for ORAISON. Cross the spectacular river bed and turn left on the D4 for DABISSE and LES MÉES.

The attractive road passes through a flat agricultural plain. In **Dabisse** watch for a tiled dovecot on the left and a lovely grove of poplars. Bypass **Les Mées** (on the left; the church has a very attractive wrought-iron bell-cage).

Follow TOUTES DIRECTIONS and then SISTERON on the D4.

You pass the **Rochers des Mées**★ on the right (☺🄰). Some of these weirdly-eroded rocks (photograph page 13) rise to 150m/500ft. Unfortunately, there is no shade at the picnic area. The road crosses the impressive **Canal d'Oraison** and then the **Bléone**.

At a roundabout (95km), keep ahead for DIGNE. At the next roundabout follow SISTERON.

Now you're on the N85 (the '**Route Napoléon**'; Car tour 4 in the *Eastern Provence* volume). You cross the fast-flowing Canal d'Oraison again and then keep it on your right. On the left, in the distance, is the large lump of the Montagne de Lure.

Just before the N85 crosses the Durance, take the D4 for L'ESCALE and VOLONNE, crossing the Canal d'Oraison for a third time.

Beyond **L'Escale** you climb above the Durance — note its stronger flow as you head north. From **Volonne** the D4 climbs to a

plateau cultivated with cereals and other crops, below a backdrop of mountains. The remains of the 11th-century Romanesque chapel of **St-Martin** stand off to the right on a hill. You crest a rise and have a fine view of Sisteron ahead. Below is the dam where the canal takes its water.

At a roundabout, take the first exit for GAP and GRENOBLE.

Once through the **Tunnel de la Baume**, you can pull up left at a viewpoint★ (☺) towards Sisteron, with its 12th/16th-century citadel rising on a sheer buttress of rock (photograph oppo͏site).

Some 3km further on, t͏ left for CENTRE VILLE, crossing t͏ Durance.

Drive through a tunnel ͏ eneath the citadel and then be͏ ͏ight on a plane tree avenue. Park ͏ ͏d stroll around **Sisteron**★ (1 ͏ m *i*🛍), a good overnight base ͏ side from the citadel, be sure to ͏ the former cathedral (12t͏ entury Notre-Dame-des-Pon͏ iers) and the clock tower with ͏ ovely wrought-iron bell-ca͏ A key staging-post throug͏ : history, Sisteron was on the ͏ Domitia linking the Alps wit͏ e Rhône Delta; almost 1500 ͏ rs later, Napoléon stopped h͏ e for lunch on his triumphal return from exile on Elba.

The next part of the tour visits the Montagne de Lure, which *can* be approached from just outside Sisteron. We do not recommend this route, however: not only is the north side of the mountain less attractive, but the road is often in *very poor* condition, vertiginous, and prone to rock-falls. We head *south* from Sisteron.

Take the N85 towards DIGNE and AIX. After about 5km bear right on the D951 for PEIPIN and ST-ETIENNE.

After passing to the right of **Peipin**, notice the necklace of low grey hillocks on the left, set off by a collar of colourful fields. Small stands of trees further enhance this unusual landscape. Beyond the vivid green fields of attractive **Les Paulons** you come to **Château-neuf**.

Bear right with the D951 for ST-ETIENNE. Pass the church on the left and then turn left for PEYRUIS on the D801, a country lane. Some 4.5km from Châteauneuf go left on the D101 for PEYRUIS.

Soon the 14th-century pilgrimage church of **St-Donat★** (♦) is seen on a wooded hillside to the right. This well-restored example of early Romanesque art rises on the site where the hermit saint (whose monks pay penance at Les Mées) retired in the 6th century.

Return to the last junction and fork left on the D101.

Now the Lure mountain is a big green mound ahead, and you pass a massive quarry.

When you meet the D951 again, turn left.

Beyond **Mallefougasse** a wide valley opens up on the left. **Cruis** is a gorgeous honey-coloured hamlet with a simple church. The beautiful valley road, bordered by

fields, takes you to **St-Etienne-les-Orgues** (150km *i* 🅿 and 13/18th-century 🏠), where some of the 16th-century houses lean out over the road. This is your last chance to get petrol for some 40km.

After passing to the right of the church with its sharply-pointed spire, go right on the D413 (D113 on Michelin maps) to climb the MONTAGNE DE LURE.

Crawl up in hairpin bends through lavender fields and then a forest of mixed conifers. About 10km uphill, not far beyond a shrine on the left, turn right along a potholed track to **Notre-Dame-de-Lure** (161km ♦☰; photograph below). This site is also associated with St Donatus, who founded a hermitage near here in the 5th century.

Return to the D413 and turn right uphill, passing a refuge on the right and then a hotel and ski-run (which unhappily disfigure the landscape in summer). At the Y-fork go either way; the roads rejoin. Now, having climbed above tree-line, you can enjoy wonderful views down off the white scree-slopes of the **Montagne de Lure★**, dotted with dwarf junipers. From a pass

Notre-Dame-de-Lure. Ancient trees shade this small chapel, built above the remains of a simple 12th-century monastery. According to legend, there was a hermitage near this site as early as the 5th century.

The Rocher des Mées, or 'The Penitents' are the subject of another legend: they are robed monks, turned to stone by St Donatus. Their crime was to lust after beautiful Moorish women kidnapped by the early 'crusaders'.

you look out toward the snow-capped Alps. The road is noticeably vertiginous now; the edge is not built up at the side. Pass the road to the Signal de Lure (1826m/6000ft) and come over another pass — to fine, if hazy, views of Mont Ventoux, the Cévennes, the Alps and the coast.

Turn round here, back to St-Etienne (193km), and continue southwest on the D951.

You pass two tiny chapels on the right, St-Joseph and St-Sebastien. The **Laye Valley** below on the left is a patchwork of colour studded with stands of poplars and low stone farm buildings.

At a fork, keep left on the D951 for BANON. Not far beyond some mellow red and ochre buildings up on the right, turn right for BANON on the D950.

The road runs through rolling hillocks and emerald cultivation. Set like a tiny gem on the right is honey-hued **Le Largue**, its tiny church weighed down by two large bells in a wall-belfry. You pass the Romanesque chapel of **Notre-Dame-des-Anges** on a hillock to the right. **Banon** is renowned for its goats' cheeses wrapped in chestnut leaves, but our other abiding memory of this village is the rainbow of shutters.

From Banon take the D51 for SIMIANE.

You cross a plateau. Rows of lavender paint attractive stripes in the landscape at any time of year and lead the eye up right to gorgeous **Simiane-la-Rotonde★** (□). Honey-coloured houses spill down the hill from the focal point — the eponymous rotunda, all that remains of the 12th-century château/dungeon of the counts of Simiane.

*The wooded D51 becomes the D22 when you enter **Vaucluse**.*

Soon the **Calavon Valley** opens up on the left — a Swiss-Alpine landscape, with rolling green hills and a lake.

At a fork, turn right with the D22 for APT and AVIGNON.

The road now follows the **river Dôa**. Soon the ochre quarries of the **Colorado Provençal★** are seen to the left, adding colour and texture to the tapestry of fields. Just opposite the D30a right into Rustrel, you could turn *left* to explore these old quarries on foot (Walk 1; photograph page 58). From here the tour makes for Apt and then Roussillon. *But* if by chance you are here on a Saturday, *don't try to drive through Apt;* take a detour via St-Saturnin to the north. **Apt** (244km *i*), capital of the Lubéron and one of the world's largest producers of candied fruits, springs to life on Saturdays, when the whole town is taken over by a vibrant market.

Leave Apt on the N100 for AVIGNON and CAVAILLON. After 4.5km turn right on the D4. Then go left on the D104 for ROUSSILLON.

Crimson **Roussillon★** (255km *i*), perched atop gouged-out ochre quarries, is one of the most beautiful villages in Provence and a fine touring base (photographs pages 60-62). Walk 2 is an easy introduction to this extravaganza of colour, best seen under a low sun.

Tour 2: THE LUBERON

Roussillon • Forêt de Venasque • Abbaye de Sénanque • Gordes • Combe de Vidauque • Abbaye de Silvacane • Cadenet • Forêt des Cèdres • Saignon • Roussillon

166km/103mi; about 6h driving; Michelin maps 81 and 84, or 245
Walks en route: 2, 3, 4, 5
Roads are varied — some narrow and winding, others wide and fairly busy. In places the road from the Forêt de Venasque to the Abbaye de Sénanque is only wide enough for one car, and you may have to back up for touring coaches. This is a good reason to set out early.
Picnic suggestions: There are delightful settings on the Lubéron, but nothing to sit on. The **Combe de Vidauque** (early in the tour) offers superb views from a rock garden of wild flowers, but no shade. As you climb to the **Forêt des Cèdres** (over halfway through the tour) you could park 3.3km uphill for superb views over Lacoste and Bonnieux; some shade. There are no views in the cedar forest on the summit, but it is cool and sweet-scented. Also **Roussillon** (see Car tour 1).

The Lubéron, a 60km/37mi-long wooded massif, stretches east to west in the cradle of the Durance between Manosque and Avignon. Seen from a distance, the range betrays nothing of its limestone crags and ravines; it rises gently off the plain in one great mass of emerald greenery. Its shape is unmistakable — reminiscent of a giant cat in slumber. Whatever time of year you climb its flanks, nature will put on a superb display: the lavender fields of Sénanque and the Vaucluse Plateau are best seen in high summer, the Combe de Vidauque in late spring, and the foothills in autumn, when the vineyards weave a tapestry of reds and golds.

Leave **Roussillon** *on the D227 (APT, ST-SATURNIN, MURS). Join the D4 and turn left (MURS, CARPENTRAS).*

The road winds through orchards and vineyards (photograph pages 4-5) but, as you reach the **Plateau de Vaucluse**, *garrigues* take over. Soon **Murs** stretches out ahead (■); a delicate wrought-iron bell-cage and the 16th-century castle with bartizans are visible.

Leave Murs on the D4 to VENASQUE.

There is a superb view left (☞) to the Lubéron, with orchards and farmlands in the foreground, just before the **Col de Murs**. Continue downhill through the oaks of the **Forêt de Venasque**. Soon you're in a grey-rock gorge , which is dry for most of the year (☎).

At the next crossroads turn left on the D177 for GORDES, ABBAYE DE

SENANQUE *(or first continue ahead to Venasque, to see one of the oldest religious buildings in France, the 6th-century Merovingian baptistery; a detour of 8km return).*

The D177 follows a more impressive gorge (best seen in autumn for the foliage), but it too is dry for most of the year. Winding down the **Sénancole Valley** through mixed woodlands, you soon have a superb view (☞) over fields of lavender to the isolated 12th-century Romanesque **Abbaye de Sénanque★** (31.5km ♠). Walk 3 passes this way; see photograph page 64. Sénanque is one of three important Cistercian abbeys in Provence, a 'sister' to the Abbaye de Silvacane (visited later in the tour) and Le Thoronet (a detour on Car tour 8 in *Landscapes of eastern Provence*).

From the abbey the road to Gordes is very narrow but, if there are no cars or coaches around, you can pull up in a passing bay for more superb views down onto the abbey's setting. At the **Côtes de Sénanque** (from where the GR6 descends to Gordes), there's an excellent view down over the plain towards the Petit Lubéron (32km ▦ and ⌂ 0.7km downhill). Now you enter the world of the 'bories' and the beautiful, incredibly-intricate drystone walls that surround Gordes (see photograph and notes page 64; Walk 3). **Gordes★** (*i*▪M) is a lively town with a good market. The plethora of craft shops attests to heavy tourist traffic. The Renaissance château (where Walk 2 ends and Walk 3 begins) houses a Vasarely museum and the tourist office. But what you are most likely to remember about Gordes is its magnificent setting when seen from the south: it rises from the plateau like an acropolis. Watch for this view: it comes up *behind you* as you leave the village (photograph page 61).

Leave Gordes following signs for CAVAILLON (D15, then D2).*

In **Coustellet** (lavender **M**), you cross straight over the N100. The Petit Lubéron rises straight ahead.

*At **Robion** go through two sets of traffic lights and, just after the second set of lights, turn left for LES TAILLADES. Beyond a mill with a working water wheel, where the D143 goes right to Cavaillon, follow CHEVAL-BLANC, staying on the D31.*

Attractive cane wind-breaks line both sides of the road, and the **Canal de Carpentras** runs along on your left.

Turn left at the signpost for Vidauque, pass a restaurant on your right and, just beyond it (by its sign) turn sharp right (500m from the D31). Almost immediately you come to a Y-fork with signs: FORET DOMANIALE DU LUBERON *and* ROUTE DES CRETES; MONTEE DE VIDAUQUE; *keep left uphill. The road ahead is one-way for the next 5.5km.*

Now climb the **Combe de Vidauque★** past various lay-bys (▦), including a fine viewpoint over Cavaillon at the foot of Mont St-Jacques (if you've ever tried to drive *through* Cavaillon, one of the largest market towns in France, you may agree with us that this is the best way to see it). The beautiful agricultural valley of the Durance glimmers below a backdrop of distant mountains. *Note:* the most impressive views of the Lubéron rising before you and the plain below come up during the first 3km of ascent, so pull up where you can before you climb too high. Almost before you notice it, the slumbering Lubéron springs to life: shaking off its green mantle, the mountain reveals rippling ribs of grey limestone. If you come in spring, you may be able to find half the entries in your field guide to Mediterranean flora on this short stretch of road. You have climbed into an unbelievably beautiful rock garden, a rainbow of wild flowers. The **Tête des Buisses** (619m) on the left marks the top of the climb (58km), and your descent begins … down the 'Rat's Hole' (Le Trou-du-Rat). *Beware: from here on this narrow road is two-way*. Sweet-scented pines perfume the dramatic approach to the Durance Valley, where bamboos, conifers and poplars shield a cornucopia of cultivation beside the turquoise river. Just before the main road, you pass a shaded picnic area with

*To visit the Village des Bories (photograph page 64), go right at the traffic lights 100m along the D2.

a lovely brook, but no tables.

Cross the Canal de Carpentras and go left on the D973. (Turn now to map 84.)

The heights of the Lubéron become more impressive again, as you head east, skirting the canal and passing the entrance to the **Gorges du Régalon** on the left.

Some 2km beyond Régalon turn right on the D32 for MALLEMORT.

Go under shady acacias and cross the Durance (look right here, to see an interesting old suspension bridge). Entering **Bouches-du-Rhône**, the road is numbered D23.

Keep ahead to the N7, then turn left for AIX (dangerous junction).

Plane trees line one side of the road, cane the other; you cross the wide **Canal EDF**.

After 1.5km turn left on the D561, then follow ABBAYE DE SILVACANE.

Beyond **Charleval** (*i*) you cross the **Canal de Marseille** (wide turquoise canals are a prominent feature of this tour, as they were on Tour 1). As at Sénanque, the simplicity of the 12th-century Romanesque **Abbaye de**

Walk 5 on the Route des Crêtes. Caves in this part of the Lubéron have been used as hideouts for centuries, most recently by the Maquis.

Silvacane★ (92km 🚶) is most impressive. St Bernard, who inspired the Cistercians, believed that saintliness could only come about through a life simply led, in poverty and isolation. All monastic buildings were to be pure in line and lacking in ornamentation. Think back to the isolated site of Sénanque; at its founding, Silvacane was equally isolated: this area was desolate, save for a 'forest of reeds' (*Sylva cana*).

Leaving the abbey, continue in the same direction. After 1.5km, go right for APT (D561). Just under 2km further on turn left on the D943 for CADENET.

Cross the **Canal EDF** and then the **Durance**, which is just a mass of pebbles here, and come into **Vaucluse**. Enter **Cadenet** (98km 🚶), where the 14/17th-century church has an attractive square 16th-century bell tower and interesting font.

Cross over the railway and keep following LOURMARIN, APT.

The centre of **Lourmarin** (*i*🚶) is bypassed. (If you turn left into this lovely village, seek out not only the 15/16th-century château, but the cemetery where Albert Camus is buried.) The vineyards, cherry orchards and stone houses around Lourmarin are particularly attractive; the limestone soil glints in the sun. Lourmarin is your next gateway into the Lubéron: from here you climb the **Combe de Lourmarin**, the wooded gorge of the Aigue-Brun River that splits the massif in two. To your left is the Petit Lubéron, renowned for its perched villages (Tour 4), to your right the Grand Lubéron, culminating in the peak of Mourre Nègre (1125m/3700ft).

After 6.5km turn left on the D36 for BONNIEUX. Exactly 3km along, turn left uphill for the FORET DES CEDRES.

The 'mushroom-stalks' of Saignon

A nominal entrance/parking fee will be collected on your ascent. Just 3.3km uphill you pass a viewpoint on the right (☎; parking for one car *only*) — a superb picnic spot, from where there are tremendous, if often hazy, views down over Lacoste (left) and Bonnieux, surrounded by vineyards. When you reach the crest (118km) the road ahead is closed to motor vehicles. This is the **Forêt des Cèdres**, and the aroma is enchanting. Walk 5 starts here, and we especially recommend Short walks 5-2 or 5-3.

Return to the D36 and go left towards BONNIEUX, but after just 300m turn right on the D232 for SAIGNON (easily missed).

This is another road with some bories, most on private property and some converted into 'bijou' residences.

At the D943, turn sharp right for LOURMARIN. Just 1.4km along turn sharp left on the D113.

A slender 12th-century Romanesque tower, all that remains of the old priory of **St-Symphorien**, is seen straight ahead.

Just past the tower, turn right for BUOUX, immediately coming to a Y-fork, where you bear left. At the next junction go straight ahead for LES SEGUINS, FORT DE BUOUX.

Take the road up right to the substantial remains shown on page 66, the **Fort de Buoux** (☐ destroyed in the 17th century by Louis XIV). When you return from the fort, head right for 300-400m to park for Walk 4.

Return to the U-turn of the D113 (about 0.6km back from the road to the fort) and bear right.

Climb steeply below more impressive rock walls draped with ivy. Beyond **Buoux** the tiny but incredibly beautiful **Loube Valley** opens up on the right (☎), then you cross over the D232 (☎ towards Apt) and wind downhill through orchards. We are taking you into Apt and then out again immediately, to give you the best view of Saignon.

*At a T-junction on the edge of **Apt**, turn right for DIGNE, SISTERON. Continue to a roundabout at the N100, then take the first right, the D48 for SAIGNON. Keep to the D48 past Saignon, first following AURIBEAU, then CASTELLET.*

You climb past ugly flats but, after another kilometre, there are fine views★ (☎) over to Saignon on the left, huddled below 'mushroom-stalks' of striated rock. The D48 turns right in front of **Saignon**, without entering the centre. You enjoy another superb view back to Saignon, focussing on the 12/16th-century church, as you climb above it. The road, hedged in by box and stone walls, now heads straight towards the Mourre Nègre. A few farmhouses with vineyards and herb gardens line the **Aigue-Brun Valley** on the right. Just before reaching the church in the lovely hamlet of **Auribeau**, the D48 turns left and snakes downhill with the Lubéron just on your right; on the left there are fine views towards St-Martin-de-Castillon on the far side of the **Calavon Valley**. Weave through **Castellet**, where burgundy-red roses spill out over stone walls. You pass the hamlet's rusty old lavender still as you leave.

*Turn left at a fork, cross the Calavon and turn left on the N100. Follow the N100 through **Apt** (AVIGNON, CAVAILLON) and, a few kilometres outside Apt, turn right on the D4 to **Roussillon** (166km).*

Tour 3: MONT VENTOUX AND
THE DENTELLES DE MONTMIRAIL

Roussillon • Sault • Mont Ventoux • Vaison-la-Romaine • Gigondas • Dentelles de Montmirail • Bédoin • l'Isle-sur-la-Sorgue (or Gorges de la Nesque • Roussillon)

182km/113mi; about 7-8h driving; Michelin map 81 or 245
Walks en route: 2, 6
Make an effort to get to Ventoux as early in the morning as possible; the heat haze builds up quickly, obscuring the wonderful views. The descent from Ventoux is a bit narrow at the start (unnerving for some drivers and passengers). No petrol from Sault to Malaucène (almost 50km on the tour). See the Alternative route on page 22 if you wish to return to Roussillon via the Gorges de la Nesque. Consider breaking the tour into two days, staying overnight at Vaison-la-Romaine.
Picnic suggestions: There are lovely shady picnic places where you can pull off the road on both the **southern and northern flanks of Ventoux**, but nothing to sit on (it can also be quite *cold* on the north side). At the bottom of the descent you pass the chapel of **Notre-Dame-du-Groseau**, the beautifully-kept chancel of an 11th-century Benedictine abbey, with stone seating round a shaded grassy 'courtyard' (parking on the left just beyond the chapel). The **Col du Cayron** in the Dentelles de Montmirail offers stones to sit on and shade. From the col you can turn right on a motorable track (behind a sign warning that you proceed at your own risk) to the Rocher du Midi viewpoint (⊼); or turn left and park below the St-Christophe chapel (see map and photographs on page 69). Also **Roussillon** (see Car tour 1).

From the *table d'orientation* in Roussillon there is an enticing outlook towards Mont Ventoux rising almost due north. The summit, a sprawl of bare white limestone scree, looks snow-capped all year round. From a distance the mountain looks much higher than its 1909m/6262ft, because it rises in splendid isolation from the Carpentras and Vaucluse plains. And when you are on the summit, you will feel on top of the world — not only because of the panorama, but because of the bitter, icy-cold winds (*vents*) that buffet the peak. Take plenty of warm clothing, in case you want to venture out of the car! Be prepared for a drop in temperature of as much as 20°F (10°C), plus a high wind-chill factor. Later in the tour, you can stretch your legs in warmer surroundings, on the nearby Dentelles de Montmirail — the finely-etched 'lace' mountains.

Leave **Roussillon** on the D227 for ST-SATURNIN, MURS, APT. Cross straight over the D4 and after 8km turn right on the D2. At the junction with the D943, turn sharp left for SAULT.

The main tour passes to the left of **St-Saturnin-lès-Apt** (♁ and 15th-century gate). The D943 travels through *garrigues*, with some fine views left over the plain, where red daubs reveal Roussillon with the Lubéron stretching out behind it. The road skirts the deep **Urbane Valley** on the left, as you approach the **Plateau de Vaucluse**. You pass to the right of the plane-shaded château of **Javon** (▯), just beside the road. This fortified building is in mint condition. Some 6km further on there is a fine view of Ventoux ahead beyond fields. **St-Jean-de-Sault**, a pretty hamlet, is the next landmark, on your left. Now Ventoux is in sight all the time, rising off the striped cultivation of the plateau, where lavender predominates (photograph overleaf).

You cross the **river Croc**; Sault rises straight ahead on a rocky outcrop. Keep following SAULT and MONT VENTOUX, to go straight through **Sault** (39km *i*▯M and last ☎ for 50km), where there is a pleasant view from the terrace of the 12/14th-century Romanesque/Gothic church and a small museum of Gallo-Roman antiquities. Sault is an important centre on the 'Route de la Lavande'. Like the 'Route du Vin', this is a marketing ploy, but a fairly well-defined swathe of blue and purple *does* extend across the Vaucluse Plateau from Vaison-la-Romaine all the way to Castellane (see *Landscapes of eastern Provence*). The cultivation of lavender was begun in the early 1900s in an attempt to slow the depopulation of this countryside; the crop adapted perfectly to the chalky soil.

At a Y-fork, go left for MONT VEN-TOUX on the D164, crossing the **Nesque**.

Some 6km out of Sault there is a fine view (🖾) back to the left, down over Sault and the cereal and lavender fields on the plateau. You start to climb through a beautiful mixed forest. In June the plumes of yellow-flowering laburnum light up the lower slopes.

Two forks are met on the ascent: go left at both of them.

Beyond **Le Chalet-Reynard** (✕▯) the excellent road climbs almost effortlessly to the summit of **Mont Ventoux★** (65km), where the *table d'orientation* is split in two halves. First you come to the southern viewpoint (🖾▯), with an outlook stretching over your base in the Lubéron and as far as the Pyrenees. Then you pass the relay station with its souvenir shop and chapel and descend to the northerly viewpoint, from where you can look out to the Alps and the coast by Nice.

From this viewpoint follow MALAU-CENE, descending the north side of the mountain in hairpin bends.

The road is quite narrow in places and not built up at the side. On the first U-bend, just to the left of the observatory, there is another fine view of the Pyrenees.

At the 'Ponts et Chaussées' build-

The surreal world at the summit of Mont Ventoux

ing, go left for MALAUCENE, to keep on the D974.

You pass a viewpoint (📷) on the right over the **Ouvèze Valley**. All the way down this side of the mountain there are gorgeous places under pines or cypresses, for picnics on *very* hot days! A better spot is **Notre-Dame-du-Groseau**, on your left after 85km (🌲). This holy place reputedly dates back to pre-Celtic times, when a nearby spring was revered; if you picnic here, *please preserve the silence and leave **nothing** behind.*

At **Malaucène** (*i*🌲🍴), the 14th-century church is built into the ramparts.

At a T-junction in Malaucène, turn right for VAISON (D938).

Vaison-la-Romaine★ (95km *i*🏛🌲M), an exquisite small town, rose above the Ouvèze as a Celtic *oppidum*, but came under Roman control in the 2nd century BC. If nothing else, visit the extensive Roman ruins. An overnight stop would enable you to take in other sights, including the museum displaying finds from excavations in the area.

Leave Vaison on the D977 for AVIGNON. After some 5km turn left on the D88 for SEGURET.

There is a wonderful view of the Dentelles straight ahead. You pass below **Séguret**, where the ruined castle rises up on the left.

Turn right on the D23 for SABLET.

Soon mellow **Sablet** is a pyramid in front of you, with its church at the apex.

Before entering Sablet, go left for GIGONDAS on the D79.

Gigondas is famous for its red Grenache wine.

Take the road left for LES FLORETS.

The lovely road climbs through vineyards towards the **Dentelles de Montmirail★**. Continue beyond the end of the tarmac; 0.7km of rough track takes you to the **Col du Cayron** (113km), at the foot of the Dentelles Sarrasines, the most northerly of the two chains and the 'lacier'. Walk 6 starts here and takes you up, over and round the crests. Short walk 6 is particularly rewarding and would take you to the rock pillars shown on page 69 in just half an hour.

Return the way you came and, from Gigondas, keep following VACQUEYRAS.

You pass several *dégustations* and areas with picnic tables (⊼).

*Go straight through **Vacqueyras** on the D7 for CARPENTRAS.*

Continuing south, you pass the lovely Romanesque bell tower of **Notre-Dame-d'Aubune** (⛪).

Fork left on the D81 for BEAUMES.

At the T-junction turn left into **Beaumes-de-Venise** (🍴). Keep the church on your left.

Just past the church, turn left on the D90 for LAFARE. You will now follow the D90 all the way to Malaucène.

You pass a pretty chapel on the right. In **Lafare** continue straight ahead for SUZETTE. Along this stretch there are several good viewpoints back to the Dentelles (📷): just past a turn-off left to Châteauneuf, pull up on the right to see the two parallel ridges side-on. From this angle the Grand Montmirail (on the left) looks just as razor-sharp as the Dentelles Sarrasines. This view is at its best early in the day, but makes a dramatic afternoon silhouette. Go through **Suzette** and turn left for MALAUCENE. Some 4km along you come to the **Col de la Chaîne**

(📷; '472m' on the Michelin map). From here there is another superb side-on view back to the Dentelles and ahead to the lower flanks of Ventoux. Descend across a many-hued palette of cultivation, heading straight for Ventoux, until you come back to **Malaucène** (139km).

Follow CENTRE VILLE through the plane-shaded esplanade and then keep straight ahead on the D938 for BEDOIN and CARPENTRAS (where Ventoux is signposted to the left). Just 3km past the sign denoting the exit from Malaucène, turn left on the D19 for BEDOIN.

Beyond a small lake on the right, you climb past clipped hedges and umbrella pines to a grassy moorland. Under 3km along the **Belvédère du Paty** comes up on the right (📷): from here you look out over the plain, with the Lubéron (left) and the Alpilles (right) in the distance. Ventoux is ahead and to the left. Below, at picturesque Crillon-le-Brave, the clay quarries exude ochre hues. **Bédoin** (151.5km *i*⛪), a gorgeous small perched village, has an 18th-century classical church. From Bédoin the main tour heads south to l'Isle-sur-la-Sorgue, but see the Alternative route overleaf if you prefer to return to Roussillon via the Gorges de la Nesque.

Follow CARPENTRAS through Bédoin, heading south on the D974.

You pass the large Ventoux wine co-operative.

Some 5.5km from Bédoin go left for MAZAN.

In **Mazan** (*i*⛪) it is worth stopping to visit the 12th-century church, where there is a wall built from 62 sarcophagi which once lined the Roman road between Sault and Carpentras.

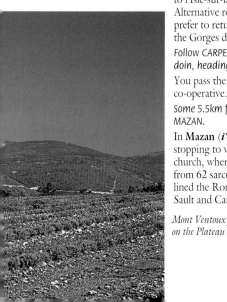

Mont Ventoux from the lavender fields on the Plateau de Vaucluse

The Fontaine de Vaucluse (see Car tour 4), where the beautiful Sorgue River gushes from its source underground

From Mazan follow PERNES (D1).

Climbing out of the **Auzon Valley**, pull over to enjoy fine views back to the Dentelles, Ventoux, and east to the Montagne de Lure. The road crosses the D4 and then the **Canal de Carpentras**. **Pernes-les-Fontaines** (172km *i*✝) is a charming small town with many fountains, an 11th-century church, and a chapel, bridge and gate dating from the 16th century.

From Pernes follow L'ISLE-SUR-LA-SORGUE (D938).

You cross the **Nesque** immediately. **L'Isle-sur-la-Sorgue**★ (182km 17th-century ✝ and *i*) is one of our favourite towns, on account of the beautiful teal-green Sorgue River, the plane tree avenues, and the lovely old water wheels. There were once 10 wheels in this pulsating mill town.

GORGES DE LA NESQUE: ALTERNATIVE ROUTE BACK TO ROUSSILLON

Continue through Bédoin on the D19; outside the village, ignore the D974 climbing Ventoux from the south; keep on the D19 to **Flassan**, *an ochre-coloured village. Leave Flassan on the D19 for VILLES-SUR-AUZON. In* **Villes** *carefully follow SAULT PAR ROUTE TOURISTIQUE, GORGES DE LA NESQUE (D942).*

The attractive *but sometimes narrow* road travels through holm oaks and manicured box hedges (⊼) above the deep **Gorges de la Nesque** on the right. Fold after fold of mountain creeps out of hiding in the gorge ahead. About 12km from Villes you look towards the most impressive part of the gorge, where high vertical grey-rock walls rise sheer from the river. From now on there is a good run of *belvédères* (📷); the best are after the first and third tunnels — from the latter you look across to the massive abutment of the **Rocher du Cire** and up the gorge towards Mont Ventoux. Beyond here the gorge flattens out into the verdant swathe of the Nesque Valley.

Pass below a 12th-century tower at **Monieux** and keep right for SAULT, crossing the plateau, a tapestry of lavender and cereals.

On meeting the D1 left to Villes, head right into **Sault**; *then follow ST-SATURNIN, to return to* **Roussillon** *on your outgoing route (231km).*

Tour 4: THE THREE-STAR ROUTE

L'Isle-sur-la-Sorgue • Fontaine-de-Vaucluse • Oppède-le-Vieux • Bonnieux • Avignon • Pont du Gard

124km/77mi; about 4h driving; Michelin map 81 or 245
Walks en route: 7. Walks 4, 5, 8 and 11 are nearby; Walks 9 and 10 are easily reached from Remoulins. *The ideal way to do this tour is to set out no later than 8am, to be at the Fontaine de Vaucluse before the crowds. Leave there by 9am and potter about the Lubéron (Walks 4-5), getting to Avignon late in the day, to break the tour. Spend the next day at Avignon and arrive at the*

Pont du Gard in the early evening. If you have only one day, you can still see the highlights of Avignon during the afternoon.
Picnic suggestions: The **Pont Julien**, a Roman bridge, is crossed halfway through the tour. You can sit on rocks beside the river Calavon; there is shade nearby. At the end of the tour the banks of the Gardon on either side of the **Pont du Gard** make idyllic picnic spots.

T his short tour takes in not only two of the most popular tourist attractions in Provence, but some of the finest perched villages in the Lubéron. *Do* set out early, to have these landscapes (almost) to yourself.

From **L'Isle-sur-la-Sorgue** *take the D938 north (CARPENTRAS, FONTAINE-DE-VAUCLUSE). Cross the Sorgue and turn right on the D25, following FONTAINE-DE-VAUCLUSE.*

You pass under an aqueduct and approach **Fontaine-de-Vaucluse★** (7km *i✝□M*). Coming into the main square, turn left to the sign-posted parking area, just as you approach the central column, dedicated to Petrarch. Now set off on foot to the famous source (shown opposite): from the column take the tarmac lane at the left of the 'Snack Bar/Glacier'. You enter a magnificent *cirque*, below which the Sorgue rushes by on your right. After a climb of 15-20 minutes, the path ends at a chaos of gigantic boulders. In summer or autumn all you will see is a tiny pool of murky turquoise water. It is hard to believe that this is one of the most powerful springs in the world! But in winter, when the vast underground reservoir in the bowels of the Vaucluse Plateau is full of rainwater, it's a different story — a deluge of emerald green water roars *over* the boulders. Linger a while beside the rushing

river, where Petrarch sought peace of mind and inspiration. When the first day-trippers snake into view, walk back to the village and take a look at the 11th-century Roman-esque church of St-Véran, the old water wheel, and the derelict mills.

Walking to the Fontaine de Vaucluse we pass this 13th-century castle and three museums — dedicated to Vaucluse speleology, the Resistance, and traditional paper-making methods. At the paper museum there is a fine viewing platform over the Sorgue.

*Leave Fontaine-de-Vaucluse by
following TOUTES DIRECTIONS from
the square. Cross the Sorgue, then
follow AUTRES DIRECTIONS until you
can turn left for GORDES PAR
ROUTE TOURISTIQUE.*

This road, the narrow D100a,
affords a good view back left to
the *cirque* above the Fontaine de
Vaucluse.

*Ignore the turn-off right to Lagnes;
continue left for CABRIERES.*

Soon come to the **Belvédère du
Tête du Soldat** on the right
(📷🚶), overlooking Lagnes just
below, the Alpilles and the
Lubéron. Further on you pass a
monument to the Resistance (🚶),
from where a footpath leads east
to Cabrières and the 'Mur de la
Peste' (see box page 64).

*At the next fork turn left, to
squeeze through lovely **Cabrières-
d'Avignon**. From here to Oppède,
care is needed to follow the convo-
luted roads. Go right and right
again immediately (where a left
turn goes to Gordes).*

The Lubéron stretches straight in
front of you now.

*At a fork, go right for COUSTELLET,
passing a shrine on the left. Cross
the D15, then turn right on the D2.*

The Lavender Museum (**M**) is on
your left here.

*Go straight over the N100 and,
11.5km further on, turn left on the
D144 for MAUBEC, MENERBES. Just
0.4km further on, go left on the D3
(MENERBES, BONNIEUX, OPPEDE).*

On the right, vineyards spread out
below the Petit Lubéron.

*Be sure to turn right, 1.5km further
on, for OPPEDE-LE-VIEUX (D176).
Then, after just 0.3km, bear right
at a Y-fork (easily missed). Cross
the D29 and go straight over for
OPPEDE-LE-VIEUX; ignore the left
turn to the village of Oppède.*

As you approach **Oppède-le-
Vieux**★ (21km 🛐🏛📷), pull over

to the right for a dramatic view up
to the ruined 15/16-century castle
and the church, with the houses
fanning out below. Leave your car
in the car park on the right and
climb through the old gateway to
the upper village. From both the
castle and the church (13th century, but twice rebuilt) there are
fine views.

*When you leave the car park, turn
right downhill, then keep following
MENERBES.*

Ahead to the right are impressive
limestone quarries. Then
Ménerbes rises dramatically before
you, spread along a ridge.

*Curve round in a U-turn below the
village, then go right for
MENERBES, BONNIEUX. At a crossroads 0.6km further on, go left for
Ménerbes CENTRE and LACOSTE.*

As you climb through **Ménerbes**★
(🛐🏛📷), fork left (EGLISE, MAIRIE).
When you come to the 14th-
century church, pull over right to a
viewpoint encompassing the plain,
Gordes, Roussillon, the Plateau de
Vaucluse, and Mont Ventoux.

*There is a Y-fork at the viewpoint:
go right. Zigzag down to a road
and turn right, then go sharp
right again almost immediately.
This is the D103, signposted to
LACOSTE. Ignore the D218 left to
Lumières, go straight ahead, then
take the next left, the D109 for
LACOSTE.*

You cross the river and pass the
road to the Abbaye St-Hilaire on
the right. The road runs through
garrigues now, and you look
straight ahead to the Mourre
Nègre on the Grand Lubéron,
with its relay station.

Come into **Lacoste** (🛐📷), where
the ruined château of the infamous
Marquis de Sade and his family
rises on the left. There is a fantastic
view over the colourfully-
cultivated patchwork of the
Bonnieux plain straight ahead.

Church at Oppède-le-Vieux

Pont Julien

Just 0.3km after entering Lacoste turn right on the D106 for BONNIEUX.

Leaving the centre of Lacoste off to your left, you enjoy a good view back to the 17th-century church.

After 2km turn left on the D109 for BONNIEUX.

The village rises ahead in a pyramid, with the church at the apex (☐). Busy **Bonnieux★** (46km *i*☀☐☐ and bakery **M**), the last of the perched villages en route, also boasts superb views — from the terrace in the centre, near the 12th-century church.

Leave Bonnieux for GOULT. (But to get to Walk 4 or 5, take the D36 south towards LOURMARIN.) Keep following GOULT but, 3.5km from Bonnieux (just past a round dove-cot on the right), turn right on the D108 for ROUSSILLON, APT. Then take the first left, go under the railway bridge, and turn left again immediately.

Park at the **Pont Julien★** (**⫪**). The three arches of this graceful 1st-century bridge supported the Via Domitia on its way south from Sisteron and Apt.

Cross the bridge and turn left on the N100, which will take you almost all the way to the Pont du Gard. Keep following ISLE-SUR-LA-SORGUE and, from there, AVIGNON.

As you approach **Le Thor** (13th-century Romanesque ☀ with Gothic vaulting) head left just before the centre*, passing the

---

*Or detour north on the D16 for 3km, to see the fine stalactites in the Grotte de Thouzon.

splendidly extravagant bell-cage over the village gate. The road follows a lovely avenue of planes for the next 3km.

At **Avignon★** (94km *i*☀⫪**M**☐) you leave the cradle of the Durance for the mighty Rhône. You will need a full day to see Avignon; if you are on a tight schedule, just climb the Rocher des Doms (viewing table). From there you can take in the ramparts, palaces, churches and bridges in one fell swoop — to say nothing of the surrounding and far-off countryside.

Leave Avignon on the N100 for REMOULINS. Where the D976 comes in from the right (after 14km) turn left for REMOULINS. The Pont du Gard is well signposted from **Remoulins** *(120km). Either follow RIVE GAUCHE (major parking area/ exhibition centre) or RIVE DROITE (parking, restaurant, shops). You can not cross the bridge by car; each entrance is a cul-de-sac.*

The **Pont du Gard★** (124km *i*⫪✕**M**; notes and photograph page 36; Walk 7) is now a UNESCO World Heritage Site. The aqueduct has been restored and the whole area pedestrianised, with exhibitions and a plethora of tourist facilities. It is *very* crowded during the day, but it has not been spoilt. Just the opposite: *the landscape has been cleared of motor vehicles and everything else that previously detracted from the monument.* If you arrive late in the day, most of the crowds will have gone. The memory of an evening picnic on the river bank would stay with you forever.

Tour 5: ANTIQUITIES AND THE ALPILLES

Pont du Gard • Nîmes • Tarascon • Les Baux-de-Provence • St-Rémy-de-Provence • Glanum • (Avignon) • Villeneuve-lès-Avignon • (Orange) • Pont du Gard

198km/123mi; about 6-7h driving; Michelin maps 80 and 84, or 245 **Walks en route: 7, 8, 11-13.** Walk 14 is just a short detour away, and Walks 9 and 10 are easily reached from Remoulins. *Good, but busy roads. To visit Nîmes and just touch on nearby Avignon or Orange, you will need at least two days. If you plan to do the tour in one day and walk as well, save Nîmes (a nightmare of roundabouts) for another day and take this pretty route: after Pont St-Nicolas turn left on the D135 and follow it via Poulx and Marguerittes to the D999. Pick up the tour again on the approach to Beaucaire. A base near the Pont du Gard or Remoulins is also ideal for visiting the Cèze and Ardèche gorges by nipping north on the N86 (even the Ardèche is only an hour away), so* we have included walks at each of these popular beauty spots (Walks 9 and 10).

Picnic suggestions: Halfway through the tour there are several picnic places with pleasant views. If you drive just 200m past the **Le Destet** turn-off, there is a shaded picnic spot on the left beside a wide irrigation canal. Perch on the side of the canal if you have no chairs. The **D24 from Le Destet to Eygalières** offers excellent pine-shaded picnic spots by the roadside. You can sit on the wall at the **St-Sixte** chapel (photograph pages 30-31; limited shade). A popular spot with local people is the pine-shaded lake just south of **St-Rémy**, where Walk 12 begins (see 'How to get there' on page 80). Also, of course, the **Pont du Gard**.

This tour captures the essence of Provence, its history, landscape and flavour. Apart from seeing many of the most impressive Roman remains in the country, we visit Glanum, settled as early as 500BC but then overrun by the Barbarians, and Les Baux, court of the troubadours. Plane tree avenues and flat market gardens hedged in by graceful windbreaks provide the perfect foil for the glaring-white limestone massif of the Alpilles. Leave the car and every footstep crushes out a new heady aroma. *Ah! Ça sent la Provence!*

Referring to map 80, leave from the left bank of the **Pont du Gard** *(the north side of the bridge), taking the D981 northwest towards* UZES. *After 3.5km go left on the* D112 *for* COLLIAS *and, under 2.5km along, turn left on the* D3, *still following* COLLIAS.

You pass a pleasant grove of poplars (⊓) and cross the **Alzon**; on the right there is a lovely weir. Walk 8 is based on **Collias**; it runs through a nature reserve on the

The Alpilles from the D24 near Eygalières

banks of the Gardon (photographs page 73).

From Collias take the D112 via SANILHAC.

You will pass a menhir on the left. In spring the young leaves of the cherry trees glow rosy-red in the morning sun.

On meeting the D979 go left for NIMES and PONT ST-NICHOLAS.

You cross the **Gardon** on a very narrow, wiggly 13th-century bridge with nine arches at **Pont St-Nicholas**, a delightful hamlet. Once over it, go left; with luck you will find space to tuck in just beyond the bridge, to admire the setting and the gorgeous green river. Then go through the Gorges du Gardon.

(Now, to avoid Nîmes, turn left for Poulx on the D135.)

It is essential to have a street plan to hand as you enter **Nîmes★** (32km *i* **ⓘ 🚉 M**). Park off Avenue Jean Jaurès, south of the Jardin de la Fontaine. First walk through these exquisite 18th-century gardens, with their fountains (in Roman times fed by water from the Pont du Gard) and the Temple de Diane. Then make for the Tour Magne on Mont Cavalier, the highest point in the city and the most impressive remains of the ancient fortifications. From the top, you can survey where you are going next — the white limestone Alpilles. Ventoux is seen in the north. When you descend from the tower, walk along Boulevard Victor Hugo, stop at the tourist office on your left, and then take in the two principal sights of Nîmes, the Maison Carrée and the arena.

Leave Nîmes on the D999, and keep following BEAUCAIRE, TARASCON at all the roundabouts.

At **Beaucaire★** (55km *i* □ **M**) the road runs beside the **Canal du Rhône à Sète** — a very attractive stretch. You may wish to see the remains of the 11/13th-century

Roman remains: triumphal arch (top) and mausoleum (left) at Les Antiques near St-Rémy; Temple de Diane at Nîmes (right)

castle (☎), which houses a museum of local history, including documents about the famous Beaucaire Fair. In medieval times as many as 300,000 people took part in these festivities in the course of one week. The fair was launched in 1217 by Raymond VI, Count of Toulouse (who figures prominently in the history of the Cathars; see box page 49). If you are not stopping at Beaucaire, continue across the **Rhône** to the twin city of **Tarascon★** (*i* ✝ ▉). The approach is magnificent: the seven towers of the massive 13/15th-century château, one of the finest medieval castles in France, rise majestically above the wide, fast-flowing river. Almost adjacent to the bridge is the 9/14th-century church of Ste-Marthe, which was greatly damaged during Allied air attacks on bridges over the Rhône.

After driving over the bridge, follow TOUTES DIRECTIONS through a long, plane-shaded square, then follow ST-REMY (D99).

Soon you can see the Alpilles ahead — slightly to the right. After crossing the N570, almost at once you come into one of those fantastic plane-tree avenues which characterise this tour. Together with cane and cypresses, they protect the market gardens here from the *mistral*.

*Watch for the sign denoting the exit from **Mas-Blanc-des-Alpilles** and, just 0.4km beyond it, turn right on the D31 (if you miss this road, turn right on the D27, which comes up shortly after). Just over 2km further on turn right again, on the D27.*

Soon you're climbing through aromatic pines and *maquis*.

Just over 4km after joining the D27, watch for a tarmac lane off right (A26a); immediately beyond it turn left on another narrow lane (A38).

After 0.6km turn up left to a *table d'orientation* ★ (☞), for breath-taking views over Les Baux and to the Camargue, the Rhône Valley, the Lubéron and Mont Ventoux. Short walk 12-2 starts here (photograph pages 80-81).

Return to the D27 and turn left.

Park at the entrance to **Les Baux-de-Provence** ★ (76km *i*☐**M**). Although at the heart of the Alpilles, Les Baux rises on a completely detached spur, with sheer escarpments on all sides; the site is extraordinary. Sadly but inevitably, today the village is so commercialised that there is no enjoyment jostling through the alleyways and ruins. If you are staying nearby overnight, try to get here first thing in the morning, although you will not be let into the ancient citadel until the gates open (9am). Walk 12 comes into the village below some of the old bauxite mines, which were opened in the early 1820s and gave rise to the modern aluminium industry.

Leave Les Baux on the D27 for MAUSSANE.

The area around **Maussane-les-Alpilles** is olive country, and Walk 13 would plunge you into the heart of the sizzling groves.

(If you want to see Daudet's mill ★, a detour of 18km return, use map 83 and, from Maussane, take the D17 to Fontvieille, then go left on the D33 in the centre of the village.

From Fontvieille you can continue 4km west on the D17 to the 12th-century Chapelle Ste-Croix and Benedictine Abbaye de Montmajour★. Return to Maussane to continue.)

The main tour heads east from Maussane, to the Alpilles.

Referring now to map 84, from Maussane head first towards MOURIES on the D17, but quickly turn left on the D78 to LE DESTET.

This is one of the prettiest roads in Provence (photograph page 85). The flat road skirts to the south of the crumpled white limestone **Chaîne des Alpilles★**. Espaliered fruit trees, olive groves, vineyards and the occasional flock of sheep in the road add character and colour to this thirsty landscape. You pass the Mas de Gourgonnier on the left, surrounded by vineyards and olive groves.

*Take the next left turn to **Le Destet** and, from there, follow the D24 towards EYGALIERES. (Or, if you are going to Walk 13 or to have a picnic, continue past the Destet turn-off for 200m, then turn left on*

the next track you come to, where there is a wide irrigation channel ahead to the right.)*

The D24 is a gorgeous pine-shaded road, bright with broom in spring, with views of the Alpilles to the left. Descending out of the pines, you enjoy a lovely outlook to the foothills, with vineyards in foreground (photograph page 26).

At the junction with the D25, turn left for EYGALIERES, keeping on the D24. (Or go right, then right again on the D25a to AUREILLE, to park for Walk 14, a splendid excursion to a Saracen tower, illustrated on page 86.)

You head straight for the Alpilles, passing several *domaines*.

Beyond the Vallonge vineyards, turn right for EYGALIERES (D24b).

Eygalières (97.5km), once a Neolithic settlement, rises in terraces on a hilltop at the left of the road. Bear right to keep on D24b; a sign reminds you that the Resistance fighter Jean Moulin sheltered near here in January 1942. You pass the 12th-century **Chapelle St-Sixte** on the right (✝; photograph overleaf), crowning a low hill. The road is flanked by beautiful Provençal farms and fields, with mountains rising in the far distance.

Take the next left turn, a narrow lane signposted to VALDITION.

You pass the entrance to this *domaine* and cross the **Canal des Alpilles**. The bamboo and

Les Baux-de-Provence, with the ruined castle at the far left. In the 13th century this fortified town was renowned as a court of love and visited by the troubadours. But in the 14th century it was in the hands of Raymond de Turenne — viscount by birth, but kidnapper by trade. When no payment was forthcoming, his victims were hurled from the castle into the abyss below.

cypresses used as windbreaks here are a delight.

Go straight over the D73e and turn left on the main road (D99).

Soon planes arch over the road — the same shady cathedral of trees that you first entered at Mas-Blanc-des-Alpilles some 15km to the west! Through the trees you look left across gentle farmlands, where row upon row of cypress and poplar windbreaks stand out darkly against the white-lace chalk of the Alpilles.

After 10km turn left for ST-REMY, GLANUM.

Although there is nothing of great architectural importance in **St-Rémy-de-Provence★** (116km *i***M**), it merits a star for its atmosphere — all light and shade, the true flavour of Provence — with plane-shaded squares, fountains and intriguing lanes. St-Rémy was founded after the destruction of Glanum, from which important archaeological finds reside in the museum at the Hôtel de Sade.

Leave St-Rémy on the D5 for LES BAUX.

You pass the tourist office on your right. If you plan to do Walk 12 or you would like to picnic by the lake shown on page 82, keep an eye open now for a turn-off right, *inconspicuously* signposted LE BARRAGE. It comes up just under 1km along. Otherwise pull up on the right 0.5km beyond this turn-off, at **Les Antiques★** (**T**), the

mausoleum and triumphal arch shown on page 27 — the surviving remains of the wealthy Roman city of Glanum, which was overrun by the Barbarians in the 3rd century and abandoned. Just over the road are the **Glanum excavations★** (**T**), covering about five acres. The area is thought to have been first settled by Celtic-Ligurian peoples (Glanics) in the 6th century BC, at the site of a sacred spring. Later building was carried out by the Greeks and then the Romans.

Return from here to St-Rémy and then head west on the D99 for TARASCON and BEAUCAIRE. (Refer to map 80 again.) After 9km take the N570 towards AVIGNON. (The third exit at this roundabout leads to Arles after 13km.)

La Montagnette, a 'mini-Alpilles', is seen ahead.

After 7km turn sharp left on the D970 for BEAUCAIRE, TARASCON; then, just 0.7km further on, turn sharp left again on a slip road (D81 for BARBENTANE).

You circle over the D970 and the railway, heading across **La Montagnette**, where pines and olives vie for space. As you climb in hairpins, an impressively-sited 19th-century pilgrimage abbey, **St-Michel-de-Frigolet**, rises out of nowhere (Walk 11). Hidden

The 12th-century Chapelle St-Sixte (right) is an idyllic picnic spot, with fine views to Eygalières and the Alpilles. Le Moulin de Daudet (below) is easily reached on a detour from Maussane.

among the buildings is the 11th-century chapel of N-D-du-Bon-Remède.

Follow BARBENTANE (D35e) from the abbey, but take the first left, the D81 towards BOULBON. Turn right when you come to the wide D35. After some 2km turn left on the D402 (MEZOARGUES, VALLA-BREGUES) and cross the Rhône.

This handy bridge in the middle of nowhere avoids Tarascon and Beaucaire and takes you to an equally handy road — the D2.

Turn right on the D2.

You skirt the Rhône, with good views to Avignon. The castellated walls of **Villeneuve-lès-Avignon★** (*i♦🏛📷*) once enclosed the summer residences of the cardinals of Avignon. Visit the 14th-century monastery (Chartreuse du Val de Bénédiction) and Fort St-André with its impressive gate. Then climb the Tour de Philippe le Bel for some of the most beautiful views on the tour, as the low sun burns out over Avignon, the Rhône and the Pont Bénézet. Ventoux is visible in the north, and you can trace all of the day's route through the Alpilles and La Montagnette.

From Villeneuve continue north on the D980 for BAGNOLS and then ROQUEMAURE.

Beyond **Sauveterre** planes and poplars protect the orchards and fields of cereals lining the road. From **Roquemaure** (13th-century *♦*) the main tour heads south, but you could go *north* on the D976 to Orange★ (*𝍤*), 11km away, to see the the triumphal arch which once stood on the Via Agrippa to Arles and the best-preserved Roman theatre in existence.

Leave Roquemaure on the D976 for REMOULINS and NIMES.

Quickly passing the chapel of **St-Joseph**, carry on through vineyards backed by low wrinkled limestone hills. You go straight over the N580, following NIMES, and then skirt the famous Tavel rosé vineyards for the next 5km! There is a viewing terrace (*📷*) at **Notre-Dame-de-Grâce**, an almshouse on your right, built on the site of a Benedictine priory. The road then passes to the right of pretty **Rochefort-du-Gard**. Soon the landscape deteriorates into suburbia.

At the N100 go right for NIMES and REMOULINS, PONT DU GARD.

Cresting a hill, you enjoy an excellent view along the valley of the Gardon towards Uzès.

*From **Remoulins** see notes on page 25 at the 120km-point, to continue to the **Pont du Gard** (198km), remembering that you can not drive across the bridge!*

Tour 6: THE CAMARGUE AND ARLES

Pont du Gard • Beaucaire • St-Gilles • Aigues-Mortes • Stes-Maries-de-la-Mer • Digue à la Mer • Plage de Piémanson • Arles • Pont du Gard

278km/172mi; about 8h driving; Michelin map 83 or 245

Walks en route: 7, 15

This is a two-day tour: on day 1 see the Camargue, then stay overnight in Arles, devoting the next day to its wealth of sights. Some roads in the Camargue are very narrow; be prepared, too, for cars in front to come to a halt without warning (the occupants have spotted some birds). The

only petrol stations en route in the Camargue are at Stes-Maries and Salin.

Picnic suggestions: Shade is hard to come by in the Camargue, and (in our experience) most areas are plagued by biting insects. If you have a beach umbrella, the daisy-encrusted dunes at the **Plage de Piémanson** make an idyllic beach setting, unless it's very windy.

The Camargue, a vast plain, is the result of a remorseless battle waged over millions of years between the silt deposits in the Rhône Delta and the salty waters of the Mediterranean. Man imposed a fragile truce in the latter part of the 19th century, when the waters of the Rhône were channelled and a sea wall built (Digue à la Mer). From the Camargue we follow the Grand Rhône north to Arles, the finest Roman city in Provence and a Mecca for van Gogh enthusiasts. Wander the alleys in the evening; with luck the lamplight will fall upon an Arlésienne in her red and white costume, her bell-clear voice singing Bizet's haunting theme.

*From **Pont du Gard** drive into **Remoulins**, then take the D986 for BEAUCAIRE.*

Skirting the Rhône, there is a view to the enormous **Barrage de Vallabrègues** on the left. See Car tour 5 (page 27) for brief notes about **Beaucaire** (22km).

From Beaucaire take the D38 for ST-GILLES.

Outside **Bellegarde** the D38 skirts the **Canal du Rhône**, before taking you into **St-Gilles** (48km *i*♿). The west front of the 11/12-century abbey church is a masterpiece of medieval sculpture. St-Gilles was home to the powerful Counts of Toulouse, who built up a vast domain and led crusades to the Holy Land. But when Pope Innocent III's envoy was murdered at St-Gilles in 1208, blame fell upon the then count, Raymond VI. He was excommunicated and forced to mount another crusade — against the Cathars (see box

page 49). As a humanist who had always tolerated the heretics, Raymond soon rebelled against these orders.

Follow STES-MARIES-DE-LA-MER to head southeast on the N572 but, soon after crossing the canal, fork right on the D179.

The **Ecluse de St-Gilles** is the lock that controls the canal between the Petit Rhône and the Canal du Rhône à Sète. Now you're in Haut or 'upper' Camargue, where desalination and fresh-water irrigation from the Rhône allow the cultivation of numerous crops, including wheat, vines, and fruit. Beyond **La Fosse** rice paddies dominate the landscape — the chief crop in the region, since it can withstand slightly salty water. At **Mas des Iscles** the D179 turns left beside the **Canal des Capettes**. The road runs into the D58 at **Montcalm** (18th-century 🏛), where flowering fields paint bold colours onto this muted canvas in spring. Some 8km further on you cross the **Canal du Rhône à Sète**.

Just beyond the canal, turn right on the D46.

From the 14th-century **Tour Carbonnière**, a watchtower on the old salt road (🏯📷), you can look out over Aigues-Mortes and as far north as the Cévennes.

Return to the D58 and turn right.

Allow at least two hours to visit **Aigues-Mortes★** (81km *i*). The fascinating (and gruesome) history of this 13th-century fortified town (when its population was almost four times what it is today and the sea was more easily accessible) will keep you spellbound. Visit the ramparts and the Constance Tower (🏯📷), and imagine the pageantry in 1248, when St-Louis embarked on his crusades with 35,000 men in 1500 chartered ships!

From Aigues-Mortes return to Montcalm and keep right on the D58. Some 5km further on, go right on the D38 for STES-MARIES.

The history of **Stes-Maries-de-la-Mer** (110.5km; 12th-century Romanesque fortified ✝★ and *i*) is steeped in legend, and for centuries it has been a place of pilgrimage, especially for gypsies. But modern-day travellers' camps being no more appealing in Stes-Maries than anywhere else, we are always glad to move on.

Drive back north on the D570.

Lime-green rice paddies glimmer along both sides of the road. At the **Pont-de-Gau Bird Sanctuary** you can see some of the nearly 400 different birds identified in the area. The **Camargue Natural**

Regional Park★ was created in 1970, partly to protect the delta from an undisciplined spread of low-grade tourist facilities; its Information Centre (*i*) is beside the **Ginès Lagoon**.

Some 22km north of Stes-Maries turn right on the D37 for SALIN.

A platform for bird-watching is passed on the right. Soon you are driving into a monochromatic landscape with no perceptible horizon; the mesmerising silvery-blue **Etang de Vaccarès** shimmers beside you. Most of this vast lagoon (the centre of the region's fishing industry and one of the most important bird habitats) lies within the confines of the **Réserve Naturelle**. (Do not confuse the Regional Park, encompassing the whole of the Camargue, with the *inaccessible* Nature Reserve now on your right — indicated on the Michelin map with dotted lines.)

In **Villeneuve** *(146km) take the D36b to the right, following ETANG DE VACCARES.*

The wide road, lined with plane trees, continues to skirt the lagoon. You can hope to see some of the famous horses and bulls here, and look out on the left for a small thatched house, built to withstand very strong winds — the traditional dwelling of the herdsman or *gardian*. Unmistakeable in their wide-brimmed black felt hats, these 'Camargue cowboys' astride white horses cut an impressive figure. The headquarters of the Nature Reserve is located at **La Capellière** (*i*).

Just past **Le Paradis**, *at a junction, ignore the left turn for Salin; keep straight ahead on the C135.*

Montcalm makes a pleasant picture in spring.

Arles: the Roman arena (left) and theatre (right).

After 4km you reach the **Digue à la Mer★**, where a sign warns that 4-wheel drive vehicles are prohibited, and *all* traffic is prohibited in wet weather. Continue ahead for 1.2km, to a pumping station, where you can park for Walk 15.

Return towards Le Paradis, but turn right just short of the hamlet on the D36c.

You pass the chapel of **St Bertrand** on the left opposite St Bertrand farm (cycle rentals, snacks).

Some 9km beyond Le Paradis go right on the D36 for SALIN.

Salin-de-Giraud (182km *i* 🚐) is the gateway to the salt marshes. Salt has been drawn from the sea here since antiquity; originally destined for the table, today's output is used in the chemical industry. Great piles of salt *(camelles)* stand beside the road, with massive Caterpillars chomping away at them (📷). The tar ends at the 25km-long sweep of the **Plage de Piémanson** (192km). You could continue by car on the compacted sand for another 3km, then walk west to the Faraman Lighthouse.

Return past the salt piles and, at the junction with the D36c, keep right on the D36 for ARLES.

This road is very busy; you no longer have the luxury of stopping in your tracks. Fruit trees, conifers, and the fine-leafed tamarisk tree proliferate on the left, but the shimmering rice paddies on the right again steal your attention. Pass through **Le Sambuc** and at **Mas de Pontèves** keep right, to continue north on the D36.

When you meet the D570 turn right into ARLES.

We would need a whole page just to touch on the highlights of **Arles★** (240km *i* 🚆🎭⛪M); it is a magnificent city.

From Arles first make for NIMES, but quickly head north on the D15 for BEAUCAIRE.

You pass a large irrigation control station. Vineyards give way to attractive fields of barley, edged by poplar windbreaks.

*From **Beaucaire** retrace your outgoing route back to the **Pont du Gard** (278km).*

Rice paddies (clos) are flooded between April and September; they make a chequerboard of glassy pools, framed by poplars.

Tour 7: LES GARRIGUES

Pont du Gard • Uzès • Anduze • (Grotte des Demoiselles) • Pic St-Loup • St-Martin-de-Londres • Lodève

177km/110mi; about 4-5h driving; Michelin maps 80 and 83, or 240
Walks en route: 7, 16, 17; Walk 8 is neaby
This is a short tour on good roads. There is ample time to see Uzès and the Grotte des Demoiselles, or to walk.
Picnic suggestions: The tables and benches beside the bubbling

Hérault at **Laroque** (halfway through the tour; ⊓) make an attractive setting. If you have time for a short walk, the ruined hamlet of **Montcalmès** is a gorgeous shady spot. This involves a 4km return detour from Puéchabon, near the end of the tour: see Short walk 16, page 89.

This tour crosses *the* Garrigues, a limestone plateau stretching from the Gardon to Hérault and forming a buffer between the mountains to the north and the vineyards of the Mediterranean basin. It's an arid landscape, sun-baked and freckled with holm oaks and aromatic herbs. Suddenly two spectacular peaks erupt off the plain and break the monotony — St-Loup and Hortus. Les Garrigues were traditionally the domain of sheep, and Lodève was an important centre for the wool industry from the 13th century until the mid 1900s.

Referring to Michelin map 80, leave **Pont du Gard** *by heading west on the D981.*

You pass the picturesque **Château de Castille** and the village of St-Maximin, both on the right. After crossing the **Alzon River** you soon see the towers of **Uzès★** rising ahead. The town (14km *i🛉🏕*) dates from medieval times. If you have time for a visit, highlights include the 11/16th-century Duché (ducal château) and the 12th-century Tour Fenestrelle, a six storey-high cylindrical bell tower.

From Uzès take the D982 west for MOUSSAC and ANDUZE.

An avenue of plane trees welcomes you into pretty **Arpaillargues-et-Auriac**, with its old stone houses, flowering balconies and classical church with lovely wrought-iron bell-cage. More planes take you out of Arpaillargues, then you pass Auriac off to the left. Once in a while a vineyard punctuates the fields of cereal crops lining both sides of the road. After crossing the **river Bourdic** you enter

another gorgeous avenue of planes.

Just outside **Garrigues** you have a first glimpse of *garrigues*. But the isolated patch of limestone scrubland introduced by this eponymous village quicky ends, and you come back into gentle agricultural land and plane tree avenues.

Just before entering Moussac, go right on the D18 for BRIGNON.

Beyond **Cruviers** the Gardon is seen on the left. Ignore signs to Ners; follow ALES, to keep on the D18.

At a T-junction, turn left for NIMES.

You cross the **Pont de Ners** (with a lovely view right over the Gardon).

Immediately over the bridge, turn hard right on the D982 for ANDUZE.

Crossing a plain, you look straight ahead to the distant Cévennes.

Go straight over the N110.

Beyond peach orchards and vineyards you come into **Atteuch**; the foothills of the Cévennes are just in front of you. Now cherry orchards take you below the 12th-century **Château de Tornac** on a hill to the left and towards **La Madeleine**. The **Gardon d'Anduze** is on your right. Continue over the railway and follow an avenue of planes into **Anduze** (58km *i*). The village is beautifully sited below high cliffs at the **Porte des Cévennes** — a gorge where two tributaries of the Gardon converge. Take a break in the attractive square, with its classical church and 14th-century clock tower.

Leave Anduze on the D133 for ST-HIPPOLYTE-DU-FORT

Beyond the 11th-century Romanesque church in **St-Félix-de-Pallières** you finally come into **Les Garrigues** — a scruffy landscape of holm oaks, acacias and pines. The road curls down to the left in front of the clock tower in **Monoblet**.

*At **St-Hippolyte-du-Fort** follow CENTRE VILLE and cross the **Vidourle**. On coming to a plane-shaded square, follow TOUTES DIRECTIONS, to leave on the D999 for GANGES.*

The **Montagne de la Séranne** stretches out to the left on the approach to **Ganges** (90km *i*). This medieval town was a silk-weaving centre during the reign of Louis XIV and still has a busy textile industry.

The Pont du Gard, one of the most beautiful and impressive monuments in the world, is in almost perfect condition, marred only by the introduction of a road bridge in the 18th century (now closed to vehicles). Completed in the 1st century, the aqueduct carried water from the Eure spring near Uzès to Nîmes — a distance of almost 50km. Where it spans the Gardon, it is the highest watercourse the Romans ever built (49m/160ft). One could sit here all day musing upon the genius of the architects who varied the span and recessing of the arches, to make them both pleasing to the eye and flexible in the event of subsidence. Even the stones protruding from the surface served a dual purpose: they supported scaffolding during restoration work, while at the same time adding visual interest. But ponder too — and with a shudder — the scene at this ancient construction site, with slaves and goats manoeuvering the massive blocks (some weighing as much as six tonnes) into position, then fixing the gigantic clamps used to hold everything together in the absence of mortar. Walk 7 is an ideal way to see the monument from all angles.

Avoid the centre of Ganges by heading south towards MONT-PELLIER on the D986. (Refer now to map 83.)

Slanting plane trees take you into **Laroque**, where an equally slanting church looks out over the **Hérault** on the right. The river tumbles over weirs (☐☐) and soon rushes, foaming, into a dramatic gorge of steep, orange-hued striated rock. Kayaks add colour to this refreshing scene.

*(To visit the **Grotte des Demoi-selles**★ turn up left 0.7km beyond the signpost indicating the start of **St-Bauzille-de-Putois**. These spec-tacular caves, hide-outs during the Wars of Religion and the Revolu-tion, are best known for the 'Cathedral' and the colossal white stalagmite resembling the Virgin and Child.)*

From the **Col de la Cardonille** there is a fine view (☐) left to a limestone ridge rising straight off the plain and culminating in the Pic St-Loup.

Beyond the col take the first left, the D1.

Follow CENTRE VILLE and ST-MATTHIEU through the flower-filled little village of **Notre-Dame-de-Londres** (☐☐). You pass the wine cooperative on the left and look right to see the 12th-century castle and 11th-century church. The D1 curls down through oaks to **Pic St-Loup**, then continues east below the mountain. From this angle the stark rusty-coloured vertical face of **Hortus**, the moun-tain on the left, commands atten-tion, while Pic St-Loup tails off on the right.

On coming to a Y-fork where the D1e9 goes left to Valflaunès (117km), turn round and retrace the road. But to park for Walk 17, continue a few kilometres to St-Matthieu (see page 92).

Heading west, St-Loup again

dominates the landscape. The ruined **Château de Montferrand** up to the left (Walk 17; photo-graphs page 93) belonged to Raymond VI, but was taken from him during the wars against the Cathars (see box page 49).

Some 5km after turning back, go left on the D122 for ST-MARTIN-DE-LONDRES.

The road runs through *garrigues* brightened by a blaze of poppies in spring. At **St-Martin-de-Londres** (128km ☐) you pass a modern wine cooperative on the right and catch a glimpse of the very pretty 12th-century Romanesque priory-church in the arcaded old town.

Leave St-Martin on the D32 for VIOLS.

After 4.5km you pass the turn-off left to the Copper Age **Village Préhistorique de Cambous**★ (☐). Beyond **Viols-le-Fort** you come to **Puéchabon** (143km). (To park for Walk 16, turn right in front of the large calvary at the far end of the village and go right again immediately.) Continue on the D32 through **Aniane**; soon planes lead into **Gignac** (*i*).

From Gignac follow LODEVE, to join the N109/E11 west.

The road crosses the Hérault on the **Pont de Gignac**★. Pull up on the right, cross the road *carefully*, and take steps down to admire this lovely 18th-century bridge.

*At **St-André-de-Sangonis**, be sure to follow LODEVE, to leave by the N109/E11. Then join the motorway north (A75-E11 towards LODEVE and MILLAU).*

Lodève★ (177km *i*☐) is a very convenient touring base. The town is very old: Nero had coins minted here to pay for the upkeep of the Roman legions. The 13th-century St-Fulcran Cathedral, which dwarfs the town with its square tower, has an impressive interior.

Tour 8: CIRQUE DE NAVACELLES

Lodève • Gorges de l'Hérault • St-Guilhem-le-Désert • Brissac • Gorges de la Vis • Cirque de Navacelles • Le Caylar • La Couvertoirade • Lodève

180km/112mi; 7-8h driving; Michelin map 83 or 240

Walks en route: 18; Walks 16 and 19 can be reached by short detours, and this route is an excellent approach to the Gorges du Tarn (Walks 20 and 21).
Some roads are narrow and winding. The road down to Navacelles is narrow ('route difficile' on the Michelin map), but wide enough for two cars to pass and built up at the side.

Picnic suggestions: As you head north along the **river Hérault**, you can picnic on rocks by the Pont du Diable (30km) or below another bridge some 25km further north (opposite the chapel of **St-Etienne-d'Issensac**). The municipal park at **Brissac** (photograph opposite) has shaded benches. The banks of the **river Vis** at Navacelles (Short walk 18, page 94) are idyllic. Near the end of the tour, the grassy slopes near the *lavogne* (paved watering hole) at **La Couvertoirade** are pleasant, but offer little shade.

This tour follows the gorgeous green Hérault River to St-Guilhem-le-Désert with its Romanesque abbey church. From this exquisite setting we continue north beside the river and then trace its foaming tributary, the Vis … to the Cirque de Navacelles — a landscape so astonishing that you will blink in wonder and disbelief.

*From **Lodève** follow MILLAU, MONTPELLIER. Cross the Pont de la Bourse and, at the T-junction, go left for MILLAU. Pass a petrol station on the left and immediately turn right on the D153 for ST-PRIVAT.*

You climb through oaks and chestnuts, with glimpses of Lodève below on the right. Beyond rolling fields of cereals, the road descends in deep shade, passing the entrance to the priory of **St-Michel-de-Grandmont** (♦) on the right and later coming upon vineyards. Dipping into a valley, a huddle of reddish-orange houses appears ahead — **St-Privat**; Les Salces sits beyond it, on the other side of the terraced valley.

*Continue through **Les Salces**, then turn left for ARBORAS (D153e). At the D9, turn right for ARBORAS.*

The road descends below the rocky crown of the **Rocher des Vierges**, with fine views right (☎) over an enormous tapestry of vineyards — the Vignoble de St-Saturnin. Squeeze through the honey-hued houses of **Arboras**

and, just before the sign denoting the end of the village, pull up right to overlook these gorgeous vineyards again (☎🍴).

*At **Montpeyroux** turn left on the D141 (ST-JEAN-DE-FOS, GIGNAC), then immediately go right in front of the wine co-operative (i). Just 0.5km further on, bear left for ST-JEAN-DE-FOS, still on the D141.*

In **St-Jean-de-Fos** the road becomes the D4.

Keep left for ST-GUILHEM and, just over 1km outside St-Jean turn right on the D27 for ANIANE, GIGNAC.

Immediately after crossing a bridge, turn right and park. There is a fine view to the 11th-century **Pont du Diable★** spanning the Hérault on your right.

Go back over the modern bridge to the D4, then turn right for ST-GUILHEM.

Now following the **Gorges de l'Hérault★**, almost at once you pass the busy **Grotte de Clamouse★**. Soon the river is just beside you on the right, a brilliant emerald green with kayaks whizzing by.

St-Guilhem-le-Désert★ (36km) lay along the pilgrimage route to Santiago de Compostela (the Chemin de St-Jacques). The 11th-century Romanesque abbey church is magnificent. (Walk 16, which starts only 10km away at Puéchabon, affords splendid views over St-Guilhem's superb setting below the Cirque de l'Infernet; see photograph page 91.)

The tour continues north on the D4; the gorge has flattened out, but the wide Hérault flows just beside the road (). Beyond a weir the road turns away from the river. In the hamlet of **Causse-de-la-Selle** follow BRISSAC and GANGES. Through the trees you can see the spine of the **Montagne de la Séranne** stretching out on the left. Some 7km beyond Causse-de-la-Selle you pass a 15th-century three-arched humpback bridge on the right; beyond it stands the 15th-century Roman-esque church of **St-Etienne-d'Issensac** (). Beyond a lovely vista of vineyards and pollarded trees, ignore the D108 right to the Grotte des Demoiselles★.

Brissac (62km) is a delight. From the village park (a left turn just past the 12th-century church with its faïence-roofed tower) you have a good view of the 16th-century castle atop the hill. In **Cazilhac** look to the right, through planes, to glimpse the attractive stone houses in the old part of the village.

Just beyond Cazilhac go straight ahead on the D25, following CIRQUE DE NAVACELLES (don't cross the bridge on the right into Ganges).

You leave the Hérault and now skirt the lower **Gorges de la Vis★** from Ganges to Madières. The Vis bounds along on your right, making its presence felt through the very wooded surrounds. Some

Park at Brissac

2.5km along there is parking and access to a swimming stretch, below a weir. Just past here, a derelict paper mill is passed at **La Papeterie**. As you climb, little hamlets with red tile rooftops keep popping out of hiding. One of them is **Gorniès**, where you cross the Vis. Magnificent conifers introduce **Le Grenouillet** (), and vertical limestone cliffs tower overhead. At enchanting **Madières** you have a choice of routes.

You can either go right for NAVA-CELLES, BLANDAS (the northern route to the cirque, with an easier access road) or you can keep to the D25 (NAVACELLES, ST-MAURICE) to approach from the south.

We think the southern route is by far the more dramatic approach. We then *return* via the north and Blandas, to take advantage of the brilliant descent overlooking Madières; this does have the slight disadvantage of repeating the 7km-long stretch between Madières and St-Maurice. Taking the southern route, you pass a small power station just below the road on the right and climb in deep hairpin bends. Just under 5km uphill from Madières, when you are almost at the top of the climb, a large lay-by (📷) on the right affords magnificent views down the gorge. Over to the left is the plateau where you are heading. At **St-Maurice-Navacelles** (93km) *turn right on the D130 for* CIRQUE DE NAVACELLES.

This road crosses the **Causse du Larzac**★, a limestone plateau peppered with box, *Cistus*, asphodels, honeysuckle and wild flowers. On coming to a farm, **La Baume Auriol** (98.5km 📷🍴), park and walk to the edge of the plateau. From here there is a breathtaking view down over the astounding **Cirque de Nava-celles**★. It is easy to see why this was one of the hideouts of the Maquis. Then continue past the farm, to descend (📷) to Nava-celles. *Take the somewhat vertiginous descent slowly; you've only a short way to go.* On reaching a T-junction (where Walk 18 leaves the road to follow a path to the source of the Vis), go right into **Navacelles**

(102km ⛺🍴; see also photo-graph pages 8-9). There is a lovely bridge here, a gorgeous waterfall, and a sprinkling of houses.

Return from the village to the junction, and go straight ahead (right) over the river for BLANDAS, LE VIGAN.

The D713 ascends the canyon, above the Vis (📷). At a lay-by 2.5km uphill, where you overlook a cedar wood, there is a *Sentier botanique* down to the source of the Vis and the setting shown on page 95 (see purple line on the map on page 94). Another lay-by under 2km further on offers a fine view back to the *cirque*.

After leaving the cirque and heading inland, turn right on the D158 for ROGUES.

Under 3km along, just before tiny **Rogues**, look out on your left for the *pink* **Menhir de la Trivalle.**

Some 0.3km further on, turn right for MADIERES *on the* D48.

You pass through the attractive

hamlet of **Le Cros**. The road, flanked by oaks, skirts a gorgeous valley on the right, then descends to superb views over Madières.

At **Madières** *go straight ahead for ST-MAURICE, crossing the Vis and retracing your route up the gorges. Back in St-Maurice (130km) cross over the D130 on the D25, following ST-PIERRE.*

This flat road zips straight across a plateau where barley is grown. A wrought-iron cross is passed on the left and then an attractive farm, the Mas-de-Jourdes. (Not far past here you might like to turn left and pop in and out of La Vacquerie, just because it is such a pretty hamlet.)

At **St-Pierre-de-la-Fage** (139km) *turn right for LE CAYLAR (D9).*

Once more crossing the Causse du Larzac, pull over right some 9km out of St-Pierre (☎), to admire the quilt of fields ahead, each patch edged by tall hedges of white-flowering ash — a magnificent

sight in early summer. Not far past here you look ahead to the dolomitic rocks above Le Caylar, where there is a cross. If you stop at the tourist office in **Le Caylar** (152km *i*), notice the carved elm in front. Go straight through this village with its old houses and clock-tower, following MILLAU. Over to the right, more fine examples of dolomitic rock spew out from Le Caylar. Just over 2.5km outside Le Caylar, as you approach the motorway, turn right on the D55 to the beautifully-preserved 12/14th-century fortified village of **La Couvertoirade**★ (159km *i*🛡). It belonged to the Knights Templar and was refortified by the Hospitaliers. Outside the village walls (a right turn from the main gate) is a fine *lavogne*, suggesting that the knights kept sheep on the *causses*.

From here return to **Le Caylar** *and head south on the motorway.* When it ends, continue on the N9/E11 back to* **Lodève** *(180km).*

*Or head north: **Montpellier-le-Vieux** *(Walk 19) and the* **Gorges du Tarn** *(Walks 20 and 21) are easily reached from Millau.*

Cirque de Navacelles from the south. Nothing prepares you for this setting: a giant cavity, 300m/1000ft deep, lies beneath you, completely encircled by steep limestone walls. At the bottom sits a hamlet, smoke curling from the chimneys. Beside the hamlet, a 'moat' encircles a tiny hillock. The 'moat' and cirque were created from the original meander of the Vis; then the river cut across the ox-bow to race straight through, a turquoise-blue ribbon tumbling over a waterfall in its haste to escape through a narrow gorge. The overall impression is of a magnificent gem in a flawless setting ... the more so in spring, when the cereal crops in the moat positively shimmer green, like a well-cut emerald caught in strong light.

Tour 9: CASTLES IN THE AIR

Lodève • Cirque de Mourèze • Mons • Olargues • St-Pons-de-Thomières • Mazamet • Carcassonne

184km/114mi; 5-6h driving; Michelin map 83 or 240

Walks en route: 22-28, (29); Walks 19-21 are easily reached from Lodève via Millau, but Walk 21 demands an overnight stay in the Gorges du Tarn.

This short tour leaves plenty of time for you to enjoy one of the superb walks en route — or, if you don't plan to do Car tour 10, to include the Pic de Nore (pick up Car tour 10 at the 138.5km-point). All the roads are good; some are busy.

Picnic suggestions: At the start of the tour there are four excellent picnic places. Just short of Octon, you can turn off left to the **Lac du Salagou** (shaded ☐; overview photograph page 104). At La Lieude you can climb to the **Château de Malavieille** (Short walk 22; notes and photograph pages 101-102); rocks to sit on; shade from the castle walls. **La Mouline** (photograph opposite), a little further on, is an idyllic setting with ample parking, but there is no shade, nor anywhere to perch. In contrast, at the **Cirque de Mourèze** (photograph page 103) you will find plenty of shade and rocks to sit on. About halfway through the tour, the **Gorges d'Héric** (photographs page 106, 107) make a fantastic setting; *allow plenty of time* and see Short walks, page 105.

Make for Carcassonne, your base at the end of this long tour through the south of France, and your gateway to the Pyrenees. Lofty castles, all different, provide the focal point. First there is a chance to climb to a ruined 12th-century château and inspect some nearby dinosaur footprints. Not long afterwards you come upon the limestone 'battlements' of the Cirque de Mourèze: while there *is* a real ruined castle here, what captures the imagination are the rock formations, which resemble ruined ramparts. Finally you reach Carcassonne — rising straight up from the plain, the old walled *cité* is a fairy-tale come to life.

Head south from **Lodève** on the N9/E11. Turn off at Exit 54, to edge the north side of the LAC DU SALAGOU on the D148.

The **Lac du Salagou** (☐) is a popular watersports centre. Three high hills jut into the lake, but seem to rise up out of it. Burgundy-red soil enhances this landscape, shown on page 104.

Pass to the left of **Octon** and bear left on the D148e for MAS DE CLERGUES. At a Y-fork 2km from Octon go straight ahead through vineyards for MERIFONS. Enter **Malavieille** 1.3km after turning off for Mérifons. Go straight through.

Just 0.5km beyond the sign denoting the village boundary, you could park for Walk 22.

Meeting the D8 at a T-junction, turn right.

Continue to the hamlet of **La Lieude**. Park on the right below the ruined **Château de Malavieille** (Short walk 22), by a large shelter housing the footprints of prehistoric animals (see notes on page 102).

Return the same way to the D148e and continue towards SALASC.

Crossing a river, you come upon **La Mouline**, the exquisite setting shown opposite. The Château of

Malavieille is visible in the northwest.

*At lovely **Salasc** take the D8 for MOUREZE.*

Soon the **Cirque de Mourèze★** rises on your left, the wonderful 'wild west' setting for Walk 23 (photograph page 103). The French have a perfect word for this chaos of dolomitic rock: *ruini-forme:* the eroded formations resemble ruined monuments, buildings, or even villages. (Walk 19 visits the most famous *ruini-forme* 'village' in the south of France.) Although very touristic, **Mourèze** (28.5km ▥) is beauti-fully kept. A ruined castle rises on vertical cliffs above the chaos; the Romanesque church (photograph page 104) is much rebuilt. Continue straight through the village. You pass a graveyard for fallen Maquisards on the left.

Turn right on the busy D908.

Soon there is a fine view of the **Montagne de Liausson**, rising behind vineyards. If you did Walk 23, you will know how easy it is — and how rewarding — to climb it.

*Pass to the left of the small industrial town of **Bédarieux** and turn left on the D909 for BEZIERS, PEZENAS. Cross the D146 and continue ahead for BEZIERS.*

(Just before entering a tunnel you can take a 3.5km return detour on the left to a *table d'orientation* atop **Pic de Tantajo**, for a panoramic view over the Orb Valley and surrounding countryside; the one-lane road is very narrow.)

La Mouline

*Go through the **Tunnel du Col du Buis** and turn right for HEREPIAN on the D909a.*

You drive under an attractive railway bridge and cross the **Orb**.

*In the centre of **Hérépian** (62km) go left on the D908 for LAMALOU and ST-PONS.*

As you follow a beautiful plane tree avenue, notice the lovely 12th-century Romanesque chapel of **St-Pierre-de-Rhèdes** (⚓) in a cemetery on your right, just beyond the turn-off for Lamalou. Some 4km beyond **Le Poujol-sur-Orb** look left for a gorgeous view over the Orb Valley, where the fair fields and green-gold vine-yards of a solitary *domaine* gird the darkly-wooded hillsides like an embroidered belt. In total con-trast, the bare peaks of the **Massif du Caroux** now rise on the right. **Mons-la-Trivalle** (77km *i*), near the confluence of the Jaur and Orb, is the starting point for Walk 24 in the **Gorges d'Héric** — one of the most rewarding walks in the south of France.

A slender 11th-century bell tower welcomes you into beautiful **Olargues★**. Beyond the railway bridge, you pass a road coming in from Le Cros on the right; Walk 25 descends it. Go through a pretty little gorge and, immedi-ately after passing a petrol station on the right, turn left to a parking area (from where the photograph on page 44 was taken). There is a fine view to the bell tower and the 12th-century Pont du Diable. Walk 25, a delightful and easy

Olargues is dominated by an 11th-century bell tower which crowns the dungeon of its old castle. The castle was taken by Simon de Montfort in 1210 during the crusades against the Cathars (see box page 49), but only destroyed under Louis XIII.

circuit above the village, starts here.

From Olargues you follow the **Jaur** through a very wooded open gorge, passing the large **Aire de St-Vincent** (⊼) on the left, in a basin overlooking the river. **La Canarie** is a large hamlet with lovely stone houses. As you near **Premian**, greenery cloaks the **Espinouse Mountains** ahead of you like a sable coat. **Riols**, with its simple Romanesque church, straddles the road.

Bear right on the N112 to ST-PONS.

Walk 26 begins at the Place Forail in **St-Pons-de-Thomières** (100km *i*✚M; see also Car tour 10), near the excellent tourist office. (Walk 29 is also easily approached from St-Pons, via the D907 south.)

Continue west on the N112 for MAZAMET.

Just beyond the D920 left to Carcassonne, you pass the turn-off right to the **Grotte de la Devèze**. From **Labastide-Rouairoux** there is a gorgeous view left to the northern flanks of the **Montagne Noire**, smothered in trees. On the right the **Monts de Lacune** make a pleasant Alpine setting of rolling green hills. Beyond **St-Amans-Soult** (where the first of the churches has an octagonal tower), you approach Mazamet via its industrial outskirts.

At **Mazamet** (135km *i*✚M; see also Car tour 10) you can take a lovely walk, full of history (Walk 27; see pages 112-114).

Leave Mazamet by heading south on the D118.

(Or, if you are not walking, you might like to go to Carcassonne via the **Pic de Nore**. See page 47: follow Car tour 10 from Mazamet. This adds only 14km to the tour, but driving will be slower.)

The D118 climbs past the **Belvédère du Plo de la Bise** (▣⊼ and seasonal *i*), overlooking Mazamet and the colourful old red-roofed factories beside the bounding river **Arnette** (one of the settings for Walk 27; photograph page 113). You pass the D1009 left to the Pic de Nore, then descend through rolling hills and farmlands (⊼). Beyond **Les Martys** you enjoy tantalizing glimpses of the **Dure Valley** on the right through conifers (⊼). Chestnut trees line the approach to **Cuxac-Cabardès**, and parcelled-up fields and vineyards blanket the rolling hills on the left.

The approach to **Carcassonne** (*i*✚M) is uninspiring; it betrays nothing of the magic about to begin. For a short time the beautiful Canal du Midi (Walk 18; photographs pages 116-117) is on your left.

The easiest way to reach La Cité is to leave modern-day Carcassonne by heading east on the N113 for NARBONNE. After 2km, just after the dual carriageway begins, turn right for LA CITE.

This road takes you to the parking area at **La Cité**★ (184km *i*✚■M; see opposite), the world's finest example of a medieval fortified town. The *only* way to see it is 'out of hours', so have dinner in the square and then wander the lamp-lit alleyways.

Tour 10: MONTAGNE NOIRE

Carcassonne • Citou • St-Pons-de-Thomières • Lac de la Raviège • Mazamet • Gorges de l'Arnette • Pic de Nore • Gorges de la Clamoux • Carcassonne

201km/125mi; 6-7h driving; Michelin map 83 or 235
Walks en route: 26-28; Walk 29 is also easily reached from St-Pons
All the roads are good, although some are quite narrow. Make sure you have enough petrol before crossing the Montagne Noire whether north- or southbound, and for the circuit of the Lac de la Raviège.

Picnic suggestions: Just under halfway through the tour the **Roc Suzadou** is a fine viewpoint over the Cesse Valley (⊼; little shade). At the end of the tour, there are ⊼ at Trèbes beside the **Canal du Midi**, or you could follow Short walk 28 from Trèbes to picnic in the setting shown on pages 116-117.

The Montagne Noire, the most southerly chain of the Massif Central, is the focal point for this tour. We move from the Minervois vineyards on its parched Mediterranean foothills to lush green highlands and magnificent forests of beech and firs. A brief foray into a more northerly range, the Espinouse, opens our way to the circuit of a lovely man-made lake. Most of the tour lies within the boundaries of the Parc Naturel Régional du Haut-Languedoc, created in 1973 to help these rural communities improve their quality of life, while at the same time preserving the environment and stemming depopulation. ('Green' tourism is encouraged, with 1800km of waymarked footpaths in the park.)

LA CITE
La Cité was first fortified by the Romans (1BC) because it lay on the road from the Atlantic to the Mediterranean. Visigoths, Franks, and successive counts carried on the work, until it was interrupted by the wars against the Cathars (see box page 49),
when the town fell in 15 days. At that time there was only one set of walls (surrounding the Château Comtal, shown in the photograph on page 115), but later in the century Louis IX added an outer wall, beyond the moat. It was then considered impregnable, but history played a cruel trick. Roussillon was annexed, and Carcassonne lost its strategic importance to Perpignan, a town closer to the border. La Cité fell into decay; there was even talk of demolition. But 19th-century Romanticism saw a revival of interest in the Middle Ages; restoration began in 1844 and is ongoing. Notice the slit-holes for archers in the walls and towers, and the wooden gallery, which allowed the defenders to hurl projectiles vertically downwards. Several towers have a projecting 'prow' on the outer side, which helped to deflect incoming projectiles and battering rams.

*Leave **Carcassonne** on the D118 for Mazamet.*

You skirt the **Canal du Midi** on your right. (Walkers could be deposited by the roadside to join Walk 28 at the Pont Rouge, where they can cross the bridge to the towpath; see map pages 116-117.)

Just beyond the Pont Rouge, take the D620 for VILLALIER.

You leave the built-up area behind; signs proudly proclaim that you are in the domain of the **Minervois** vineyards and the land of the Cathars (see box page 49).

*Keep right outside **Villalier**, following CAUNES.*

The gentle southern slopes of the **Montagne Noire** rise ahead. The public gardens at **Villegly** are a fine splash of greenery.

At a fork with the D11 bear left for CAUNES; then follow CITOU.

You pass to the left of **Caunes-Minervois** (✝), where the 7th-century Benedictine abbey was restored in the 1700s. (From Caunes you *could* take a circuitous route to Minerve, the village that gave its name to the surrounding area, and the site of one of the most horrific episodes in the Albigensian Crusade. Walk 29 explores Minerve, but is more easily reached from St-Pons.) The D620 skirts the wooded gorge of the **Argent-Double** with its rustic stone farmhouses. The Minervois is left behind, and you move from the Mediterranean foothills to the verdant north. The next stretch of the tour, from here to the N112, is the most beautiful. Notice the ruins of the château on the hill at **Citou** (31km 🄫) and then the pretty stream falling in tiers on the right. **Lespinassière** is a particularly attractive perched village (🄫🖾). As you climb out of it, stop as soon as you clear the trees: there is a magnificent view back over the village and its

restored 15th-century clock-tower. Two kilometres further on you pass a sign commemorating Resistance fighters, then enter the **Forêt Domaniale de Nore**.

Beyond the **Col de Salette** you descend to the north on a broom-bristling road flanked by undulating green hills.

At a junction turn right on the D920 for ST-PONS.

Some 3km further on you come to **Roc Suzadou** (🖾🄫), with a tremendous view over this bucolic countryside. An avenue of gorgeous chestnut trees welcomes you to the lovely hamlet of **Aymard**. At **Courniou** (63.5km) you meet the N112, where the **Grotte de la Devèze★** is almost opposite, on the road to the railway station.

Turn right on the N112.

St-Pons-de-Thomières (68.5km *i*✝M) is the seat of the Regional Park. On approaching the splendid 12th-century cathedral, park in the Place Forail on the right for Walk 26 or to visit the excellent tourist office. (The D907 south from St-Pons is the quickest route to Walk 29 at Minerve.)

Leave St-Pons on the D907 north for LA SALVETAT.

After passing the road to Brassac off to the left, keep an eye out after 0.8km for two stone gateposts and a signpost, CAMPING VERT, on your right: you can drop walkers off here for Short walk 26.

You climb into the **Monts de l'Espinouse**. Cross the **Col du Cabaretou**, coming down into fields with spring flowers, conifers and beech (🄫). Soon a hairpin-bend descent offers fine views (🖾) down over La Salvetat, at the confluence of the Agout and Vèbre.

Without crossing the bridge to enter La Salvetat, bear left, then take the second right (LAC DE LA RAVIEGE). Beyond a dairy, go left, again following LAC DE LA

RAVIEGE. Cross a bridge and go right (TOUR DU LAC).

You skirt the northern side of the lovely **Lac de la Raviège**, a water-sports centre. There is a fine view to the right (☞) over La Salvetat in the valley, below the backdrop of the Espinouse.

*When you meet the D52 turn sharp left for ANGLES, crossing the dam. Go straight through **Anglès**, following BRASSAC. At the **Col du Fauredon**, go left on the D53 for BOUISSET and MAZAMET.*

Bouisset is a stark village, enlivened only by a bright green well in the centre; in contrast, **Le Rialet** is a pretty red-roofed hamlet. Beyond here you climb into a 'cathedral' of beech and pines.

*Just after passing a small dam on the right at **Le Vintrou**, go right on the D54.*

Descending towards Mazamet, you see the 'Black Mountain' from the most impressive angle: dark granite slopes, clad with firs, rise abruptly from the Thoré plain. Follow CENTRE VILLE into the centre of **Mazamet** (138.5km *i⚥M*), then follow CARCASSONNE.

Watch for the octagonal tower of St-Sauveur on your left: 400m beyond it, turn left on the D54 for PRADELLES, PIC DE NORE.

You enter the **Gorges de l'Arnette** and soon climb hard by the river, past a series of picturesque stone-built, red-roofed leather works and woollen mills (photograph page 113). The river tumbles down over weirs beside you, and you soon drive past the few houses of **Moulin Maurel**, where Walk 27 begins and ends.

Some 500m beyond Moulin Maurel turn off left to TREBY, PIC DE NORE.

Beyond the honey-coloured hamlet of **Les Yés** the mountain views open up. **Tréby** is a forestry house where Black Mountain

troups regrouped in June 1944. You climb above beech and firs (**Forêt de Nore**) to a wind-buffeted moonscape, where a rocket-like TV transmitter beckons — the **Pic de Nore★** (1210m/ 3970ft; 156.5km ☞). The Espinouse and Lacune massifs rise in the north; in the south the Corbières and Pyrenees are visible.

Turn back from the viewpoint and, just past the relay station, go left on the D87 for CARCASSONNE.

Ahead, dark conifers pierce the bright canopy of deciduous trees. **Pradelles-Cabardès** is a holiday village in the midst of woods and flower-drenched meadows.

On meeting the D112, go left.

From the watershed of the **Col de la Prade**, you descend in zigzags back into the dry Mediterranean landscape of the **Gorges de la Clamoux**. A solitary patch of vineyards is glimpsed far below — at **Cabrespine** (173.5km ⌂), where a ruined château rises on the right. Attractive cultivation lines the gorge further downhill. A 12th-century tower on the main road at **Villeneuve-Minervois** (⬛) mimics Carcassonne with its slate roof.

Keep following CARCASSONNE (D112) until you meet the D620, then turn right and retrace your outgoing route as far as Villalier.

In this flat landscape, the table-topped hill of **Na Aurenque** on your left, with its bib of vineyards, is a pretty picture on the approach to **Villegly**.

*Back in **Villalier**, just beyond the church, go left on the D101.*

This quiet road, arched with planes, takes you straight to **Trèbes**, where you cross the Canal du Midi (🚍; Short walk 28).

*From Trèbes follow CARCASSONNE, taking the N113 back to **La Cité** (201km).*

Tour 11: CORBIÈRES, LAND OF THE CATHARS

Carcassonne • Lagrasse • Château de Quéribus • Duilhac-sous-Peyrepertuse • Gorges de Galamus • Couiza • Limoux • Carcassonne

195km/121mi; about 7h driving; Michelin map 86 or 235
Walks en route: 28, 30-34, (35), 36

There are quite a few narrow roads; the short stretch to the Château de Peyrepertuse (a detour) and the road in the Gorges de Galamus are especially difficult if you meet on-coming traffic. The longest stretch without petrol is between Lagrasse and Rouffiac (72km). If you have time for a two-day tour, see Car tour 12: you can head south from the Grau de Maury towards the Pyrenees, perhaps breaking your journey within sight of Canigou.
Picnic suggestions: *Early in the tour, at Termes, there are two idyllic settings (see Short walks on*

page 122 and photographs on page 123). Halfway along, at the **Grau de Maury**, *two trees by a stone shelter provide the only shade for miles around, and there is a fine view over to Quéribus. A little further along, you can get to the* **banks of the Verdouble** *by turning right before Duilhac (just past the bridge; see map pages 126-127). After 2km park in a turning area. Cross the river on a foot-bridge (or ford, if the bridge is washed away) and walk up the 'marble river bed' shown on page 125, to the waterfalls. Just beyond* **Bugarach**, *near the end of the tour, you could picnic by the bridge shown on page 132 (see Short walk, page 131).*

This tour winds up into the Corbières, last great strong-hold of the Cathars. Bounded on the north by the Aude, this upland region rises between the Montagne Noire (Car tour 10) and the Pyrenees. Up until the conquest of Roussillon from Spain, the Corbières were of great strategic importance to France as a bulwark against the kingdom of Aragón. After the fall of the Cathars at Carcassonne, Louis IX fortified La Cité and five more sites in the Corbières — Puilaurens, Peyrepertuse, Quéribus, Termes and Aguilar. These castles, recaptured Albigensian strongholds, became known as the 'five sons of Carcassonne'. With the annexation of Roussillon in 1658 these fortresses lost their strategic importance and fell into ruin, as did Carcassonne.

From **Carcassonne** *take the N113 east. Just as you enter* **Trèbes**, *turn right on the D3 for LAGRASSE.*

Some 5km along, a green basin of vineyards below a hill opens up ahead. A land of *garrigues* inter-spersed with hard-won vineyards, the **Corbières** yield a rich and fruity wine with a high alcohol content. The vines luxuriate on this calcareous soil; the Romans cultivated the grape in this region. Beyond **Monze, Pradelles-en-Val** and **Villemagne** you come into the heavily-wooded **Gorges de**

l'Alsou (⌂ with fireplaces). On entering **Lagrasse★** (34km *i⌂▮*; Walk 30, notes pages 120-121) look right as you cross the bridge over the **Orbieu**, to see the 11th-century bridge and 8th-century abbey. Wander the alleys of this gorgeous fortified village, not missing the 13th-century covered market or the highly-decorated 14th-century church.

At the junction 3.5km outside Lagrasse, bear right on the D23 for TALAIRAN, CHATEAU DE TERMES. Almost immediately keep straight

The Château de Peyrepertuse, rising above Rouffiac (Walk 32)

LAND OF THE CATHARS

Wherever you drive in this part of southwest France, you will see signposts proudly proclaiming that you are in the land of the Cathars. Catharism, a doctrine of 'purity', took hold in the Languedoc in the early 12th century, in great part as a reaction against the excesses of the church of Rome. Centred on Albi, its adherents (also called Albigensians) fanned out to the south and east, and soon boasted their own bishops and strongholds, including Carcassonne. They counted among their adherents wealthy merchants, artisans and professional people. At this time the Languedoc was in the hands of the Counts Raymond of Toulouse, humanists who tolerated this heretical sect. But the Cathars were a thorn in the side of Rome, and their success led to their eventual downfall. When his envoy was assassinated near St-Gilles (Tour 6) in 1208, Pope Innocent III determined to destroy the heretics. A 'crusade' was mounted. First Béziers fell, then Carcassonne. Although the wars intensified from 1210, under Simon de Montfort's 'scorched earth' policy, only in 1229 was a truce imposed. Even then a few pockets of resistance remained. It took the Inquisition and the burning to death of 200 Cathars at Montségur in 1244 to eradicate the scourge of the 'pure ones'. The kings of France were only too happy to help Rome suppress the sect; they saw the great spoils to be gained. In 1271 Languedoc was officially annexed to France.

ahead (same signposting), then quickly turn right on the D212 for ST-PIERRE, CHATEAU DE TERMES. Beyond **St-Pierre-des-Champs** you follow the sinuous Orbieu through a gorge. A lovely little Romanesque church stands on the right as you skirt honey-hued **St-Martin-des-Puits**. The mountains become more prominent now, and you pass below the ruins of the **Château de Durfort** (⬜), rising above a meander of the river on the left. This château was abandoned without a fight on the arrival of de Montfort.
Just after circling Durfort, go left for TERMES on the D40.
The **Gorges du Terminet**, a chaos of rock and holly oaks, now lead you to flower-filled **Termes** (55.5km ⬜; Walk 31; photographs page 123 and overleaf), where the

château rises on your right. From Termes the D40 continues south along a crest between two wooded ravines. The tabletop Montagne de Tauch, with its tower, dominates the landscape to the southeast. Notice the creative topiary of the box hedges at the side of the road.

*At the **Col de Bedos** turn left on the D613 for FELINES.*

Over to the right there is a gentle valley backed by mountains. In spring this stretch is awash with golden broom and white-flowering false acacias.

*Just after entering **Félines**, turn sharp right on the D39 for TUCHAN. Then go right again on the D139 for DAVEJEAN and MAISONS. In the centre of **Davejean** turn sharp left on the D10 for MAISONS. Climb*

49

*above Davejean and in under 2km (at the **Col du Prat**), go left on the D410. At the end of **Maisons** head south on the D123 for PADERN. Then, less than 2km further on, go sharp left for PADERN (still D123).*

You head straight for the **Montagne de Tauch**. Considering the foothills that have gone before, you're in impressive mountains now. The road skirts the gorges of the **river Torgan** all the way to **Padern** (84km ⧖), where another ruined castle on the left dominates the village. After crossing a bridge over the Verdouble, you reach a junction with the D14. (Here you could turn left for a detour through the Fitou vineyards to Tuchan and from there go on to the 13th-century Château d'Aguilar (▮) — or to Ségure, for Walk 35.)

The main tour turns right on the D14, towards CUCUGNAN.

You head southwest along the **Verdouble Valley** — towards a spike of pale grey rock crowned by the château of Peyrepertuse. For Walk 34, park just below the red and honey cluster of **Cucugnan**.

Just past Cucugnan, turn sharp left uphill on the D123 for MAURY.

Some 2km uphill, at the **Grau de Maury**★ (⧖), turn left and climb to the parking for the **Château de Quéribus**★ (93km ⧖; see notes for Walk 34 on page 127). From here the whole plain of Roussillon is at your feet, with Canigou rising in the Pyrenees as a centrepiece. Nearby, in the northwest, the silhouette of Peyrepertuse blends so well into a limestone ridge that it is hardly perceptible. On the descent from the castle there is a fine view of the Verdouble and Cucugnan valleys.

*Back at the **Grau de Maury** (shaded picnic spot straight ahead), turn right, back towards CUCUGNAN. (Or, if you are taking an extra day to see the Pyrenees,*

turn left and refer to the notes on page 52.) At the junction with the D14 turn left.

You head west through the most intensively-cultivated stretch on the tour. Vineyards sweep away on both sides of the road, fringed by wooded slopes below white limestone crags.

*At the entrance to **Duilhac-sous-Peyrepertuse** (101km)* keep straight ahead for ROUFFIAC on the D14.*

Park near the *auberge* in Duilhac for Walk 33; park at the **Col de Grès** 3km past Duilhac for Walk 32. If you need petrol, turn off right into the centre of tiny **Rouffiac-des-Corbières** (🛱), a delightful flower-bound hamlet (where you could also park for Walk 32). Otherwise continue straight ahead (with fine views up left to Peyrepertuse). Notice the tangerine-coloured stone of the simple church at **Soulatge**. Little parcelled gardens hide behind the stone walls at **Cubières-sur-Cinoble** (115km).

In Cubières, turn left on the D10 for ST-PAUL-DE-FENOUILLET.

This *very narrow* road climbs through the **Gorges de Galamus**★. Although the gorge is not very long, its high vertical white rock

---

*If you are not doing Walk 32, but you wish to visit the 3rd-century **Château de Peyrepertuse**★, take the *very narrow, vertiginous* road at the entrance to Duilhac *(a detour of 7km return; plus 1h return on foot)*. This largest of the 'sons of Carcassonne', with ramparts over 300m/1000ft long, covered an area equal in size to the Cité of Carcassonne! This Cathar stronghold was so inaccessible that even de Montfort dare not lay siege to it. Peyrepertuse was the base for a final attempt to retake Carcassonne (1240); when this failed the castle fell to the royal army without a battle.

walls make it one of the most impressive gorges in the eastern Pyrenees. Park 4km along, just before a tunnel. Take the path and long flight of steps down to the hermitage **St-Antoine-de-Galamus** (♠✗▣), to admire the fine view over the most impressive part of the gorge. (Just beyond the tunnel there is another parking area with a view to the hermitage and a wine-tasting kiosk, but it's a longer walk to the chapel.)

Return to Cubières and turn left on the D14.

The road now follows the **Agly Valley**, a beautiful swathe of green and gold cultivation. Soon you pass to the right of the **Pech de Bugarach★** (1230m/4035ft; Alternative walk 36, photograph page 132), the highest mountain in the Corbières. Beyond the village of **Bugarach** (park near the *mairie* for Walk 36 or 2km further on for Short walk 36), you follow the wooded gorge of the river **Blanque**. It bounds along beside you at **Rennes-les-Bains**.

Just 3km beyond Rennes turn left on the D613 for COUIZA.

At **Couiza** (151km ▮), there is a well-preserved château and bridge (both 16th century).

Go right on the D118 for LIMOUX.

The road bypasses the centre of **Alet-les-Bains** (ruined 11th-century ♠) and comes into **Limoux** (166km *i*♠), known for its carnival and sparkling wine (*blanquette*).

Follow CARCASSONNE, but watch for your fork right for PIEUSSE and ST-HILAIRE.

You cross the Aude again and can look right to see the old 15th-century bridge and spire of the 13/16th-century Gothic church. Unfortunately there is nowhere to pull up to enjoy this view.

Turn left on the D104 for PIEUSSE and ST-HILAIRE.

Just over 1km along you pass the Gothic pilgrimage chapel of **Notre-Dame de Marceille** on the left. **Pieusse**, another outpost of the Cathars, is bypassed, and you descend to **St-Hilaire** (♠) in a cradle of vineyards, passing to the right of the Romanesque/Gothic church and 14th-century cloister. It was the Benedictine monks of St-Hilaire who reputedly discovered the secret of *blanquette*. After crossing the river **Lauquet**, the road bypasses the centre of **Verzeille** and comes into **Leuc**.

Head left for COUFFOULENS but, at a Y-fork under 2km further on, bear right for CAVANAC (D304).

You come over a hill and look down on the plain of Carcassonne.

Turn left on the D142. Just after passing under the motorway, turn right (D104, CAMPING DE LA CITE).

Soon you have a brilliant view of **La Cité** (195km), especially attractive at twilight.

The gorgeous village of Termes, on the banks of the Orbieu. Walk 31 is a beautiful circuit, which can include a visit to the château. The building, shown on page 123, fell to de Montfort in 1210 after a siege of four months and was later fortified by St-Louis.

Tour 12: TOWARDS THE PYRENEES

Château de Quéribus • Castelnou • St-Michel-de-Cuxa • Villefranche-de-Conflent • St-Paul-de-Fenouillet • Quillan

206km/128mi; about 5-6h driving; Michelin map 86

Walks en route: 34 (as a circuit from Quéribus); 36 (if returning via the Gorges de Galamus)

This tour follows many narrow and winding roads; there are also short stretches on the N116 'raceway'.

Picnic suggestions: About two-thirds of the way through the tour, a ruined farm on the D619 north of Catlar (near the **Pic de Baou**) offers ample shade and rocks to sit on. Some 10km further on, at the **Roman aqueduct at Ansignan**, you could sit on the aqueduct or under it; the arches provide the only shade.

This tour is an ideal companion to Car tour 11 and an excellent gateway to the eastern Pyrenees. If you like what you see, then *Landscapes of the Pyrenees* will take you across the range, to the Atlantic coast.

From the **Grau de Maury** take the D19 south. Leave **Maury** (*i*), with its huge wine cooperatives, on the D117 east for ESTAGEL, PERPIGNAN. In the centre of **Estagel** turn right on the D612 for MONTNER/MILLAS. At the **Col de la Bataille** turn left uphill (the road is not built up at the edge, but is amply wide).

After 4km park on the right, at the hermitage of **Forca Réal★** (*☗*), from where there is a superb view over the plain and the coast. Inland, Quéribus rises like a needle from the crests and, further west, the Pech de Bugarach can be recognised by its two distinct peaks. As you descend from the hermitage, there is a superb view over the Pyrenees villages south of the N116, with Canigou behind them.

Back at the col, turn left. After 5km turn right and cross the river **Têt**, to enter **Millas** (36.5km). In the centre, turn left on the N116 for PERPIGNAN but, after only 0.6km (just after crossing the river **Boulès**) turn right on the D612 for THUIR. After crossing the D16 signposted right for Corbère, take the next right, the D58 for CAMELAS.

In early summer the peach trees along this road are heavily laden.

After 2km turn left on the D615, then go right immediately for CASTELNOU.

A narrow road takes you to **Castelnou★**, straddling a knoll in a green basin (*▣*). This wonderfully picturesque medieval Catalan village is a beehive of molasses-coloured stone and salmon roofs, surrounded by a bib of vineyards.

Follow CAIXAS to leave Castelnou on the D48.

The summit of Canigou is straight ahead; in the middle distance the chapel of St-Martin rises across the valley, on a mountain to your

View to Canigou from the ruined farm near the Pic de Baou

St-Michel-de-Cuxa, where for many years Pablo Casals took charge of the Prades music festival. Canigou rises behind the abbey, its summit snow-capped for much of the year. One of most important religious buildings in the south of France, the 10th-century abbey was founded for the Benedictines. During the Revolution, parts of the building (at that time abandoned) were sold; later a good number of the original columns found their way to the banks of the Hudson River in New York (as did the cloisters of St-Guilhem-le-Désert, visited in Car tour 8). Today the abbey is under the care of Cata-lonian monks from Montserrat; set in peach tree orchards, it almost has the appearance of a domaine.

right. Behind it is the omnipresent Quéribus.

When you meet the D2, turn sharp right for ST-MICHEL-DE-LLOTES.

The isolated chapel of **Fontcou-verte** (⚱) stands off to the right here in a desolate landscape. Drop down in hairpin bends to **St-Michel-de-Llotes** and pass below its Romanesque church on the right.

Continue towards BOULETERNERE on the D16.

Peach, cherry and plum trees line the road to **Bouleternère**, where a Romanesque church rises at the top of the village.

Follow VINÇA and PRADES (D16), then turn left on the N116.

After 4km you pass the **Barrage de Vinça** (⌂), with a Roman-esque chapel. The road bypasses Vinça, where there is a lovely Romanesque church tower. After crossing the river **Lentilla** you come into **Marquixanes**, where there is another Romanesque church tower on the left. Now, if you have *Landscapes of the Pyrenees* and plan to climb Canigou, take either of the next two roads on the left (D24, D24b for Villerach).

In **Prades** (84.5km *i*) follow CENTRE VILLE, then leave on the D27 for CODALET, TAURINYA.

This road takes you past the **Abbaye St-Michel-de-Cuxa★** (⚱) and then the attractive 11th-century Romanesque church in **Taurinya**, to the **Col de Millères**. You pass the ruined Romanesque **Tour de Cours** on the right.

Just before the centre of **Fillols**, *fork right for CORNEILLA (D47).*

Soon the village is visible in the valley, below a high red escarp-ment. Curl down into **Corneilla-de-Conflent** (⚱) and squeeze between the square tower of the fine 11/12th-century Romanesque church on your right and a round tower on the left. Continue to the beautiful medieval village of **Villefranche-de-Conflent★** (114km *i*⚱▮), and visit the 12th-century church of St-Jacques and the ramparts. First fortified by Spain to confront the 'five sons of Carcassonne', some of the original 11th-century walls remain, but the ramparts are chiefly the work of Vauban (17th century).

Leave on the N116 for PRADES and, beyond **Ria**, *follow PERPIGNAN on the ring road, until you can leave it for CATLAR (D619). Go through* **Catlar**, *cross the* **Castellane** *and, 1km further on, turn sharp right on the D619 for SOURNIA.*

There are magnificent views to Canigou as you climb this narrow road through *garrigues* — the mountain is visible from top to bottom, rising from the plain. Some 10km along you come to a deserted farm on the right, where you can picnic in the setting shown opposite (☞), the *only shade* in these sun-drenched

The Roman aqueduct over the river Agly at Ansignan

garrigues. Some 2km past here, at the **Pic de Baou/Col de Roque Jalère** (📷), there is just room to pull over on the right and look north over the huge basin of the Fenouillèdes, with the Corbières range and the Château de Peyrepertuse in the distance. The wedge of the Pech de Bugarach rises to the west of Sournia, which is seen below. Pass the oddly-shaped **Roc Cornut** on the left and keep ahead for SOURNIA. A quarry rises behind unremarkable **Sournia** (128km 🍴).

At the T-junction turn right on the D619 for ST-PAUL. Almost immediately, go right for PEZILLA (D619). After 4km go left for PEZILLA.

Stone-walled terraces enhance the approach to **Pézilla-de-Conflent**, where a Romanesque tower rises on the left above the red rooftops.

*At a fork 3km beyond Pézilla, keep ahead on the D619 for ANSIGNAN. Just past the entrance to **Ansignan** turn right on the D9 for TRILLA.*

A lovely view over vineyards opens up on the left; they hide a treasure.

Under 1km further on, turn sharp left downhill on a very narrow lane (small signpost, AQUEDUC). Cross a stream and then turn left again.

Soon you see the aqueduct★ (📷) shown above, spanning the **Agly**.

*Return to **Ansignan** the same way, then turn right for ST-PAUL (D619).*

The high limestone crags of the most southerly Corbières rise just in front of you as you follow the wooded Agly gorge. You cross a bridge in a very pretty setting, with the ruins of an old Roman bridge ahead. In **St-Paul-de-Fenouillet** (153km) you have a

54

choice; distances for both routes are approximately the same. Either go north through the GORGES DE GALAMUS★ and pick up Car tour 11 in **Cubières** (the 115km-point), or go via QUILLAN and join it at **Couiza** (the 151km-point).

*To go via Quillan, leave St-Paul on the D117 for FOIX, crossing the Agly. Pass through the outskirts of **Caudiès-de-Fenouillet** and, 6km further on (just after crossing the river **Boulzane**), turn left on the D22 for PUILAURENS.*

The crenellated silhouette of the château soon towers above you in a dramatic setting, with the river on the left. In **Puilaurens** turn right on a good road to the **Château de Puilaurens** (📷; 45min return on foot). This Cathar stronghold became the 'son of Carcassonne' closest to Aragón.

Return to the D117 and turn left for QUILLAN.

Skirting the river **Aude** (🍴), you bypass Axat, then cross the Aude and follow the narrow **Défilé de Pierre-Lys**, where the river threads through limestone cliffs (🍴). This is a main road used by lorries but, when you can, pull over to look at the rushing river and take in some negative ions. The lovely old part of **Belvianes** is seen off to the right, then the Aude spills over a weir. The wide moss-green river and the plane-shaded road enhance the approach to **Quillan** (194km *i*). A thriving market and manufacturing town, Quillan is also a good walking base. (From here Cathar devotees can take a detour west on the D117 to the imposing ruins of the Château de Puivert; 32km return.)

*From Quillan take the D118 for LIMOUX. Still skirting the Aude, you join Car tour 11 at **Couiza** (206km).*

❀ Walking

Those who go to France purely for a walking holiday are likely to be tackling the long linear GR routes. *This book has been written for motorists who want to tour the most beautiful roads and enjoy some glorious walks en route.* Very few of the walks are strenuous, and we don't include hikes to summits that are easily reached by car (like Ventoux). The walks have been chosen to highlight the great variety of landscapes in the area and to focus on our favourite beauty spots.

Although the walks are scattered between Aix and the Pyrenees, you should find many within easy reach (no more than an hour away by car or public transport) no matter where you are based. If you are staying in one area for a couple of weeks, visit the nearest *syndicat d'initiative* (tourist office) to get information about local walks and up-to-date **bus and train timetables** (some of our walks are accessible by public transport; see 'How to get there' at the top of the relevant page and transport information on the touring map).

Weather

All the walks in this book may be done the year round, but from mid-June to mid-September it will be far too hot to enjoy any but the easiest rambles. *Moreover, areas prone to forest fires (the Alpilles, for example) may be closed to visitors from mid-July until mid-September.* Spring and autumn are the best seasons for walking; not only are the temperatures moderate, but there is an extravaganza of wild flowers and seasonal foliage. On the other hand, you will have to put up with a few days of torrential rain. In winter the landscape is more monotone, but the weather is usually dry, clear and cool. The notorious *mistral* blows for about a third of the year (usually in winter and spring and usually for a *minimum* of three days). Often it is difficult to stand upright, and no walks should be attempted in areas exposed to this northerly wind.

What to take

No special equipment is needed for any of the walks, but proper **walking boots** are preferable to any other footwear. Most walks in the south of France cross very stony terrain at some stage, and good ankle support is essential. In wet weather you will also be glad of the waterproofing. A **sunhat** and high-protection **suncream** are equally important;

there is a real risk of sunstroke on some walks. Each member of the party should carry a small rucksack, so that the chore of lugging the essentials is shared. *All year round* it is advisable to carry a first-aid kit, whistle, torch, spare socks and bootlaces, and some warm clothing (the *mistral* can blow up suddenly, with temperatures dropping up to 10°C/20°F!). A long-sleeved shirt and long trousers should be worn or carried, both for sun protection and for making your way through the prickly plants of the *maquis.* Depending on the season, you may also need a windproof, lightweight rainwear, woollies and gloves. Optional items include swimwear, a Swiss Army knife, mobile phone, insect repellent. Mineral water is sold almost everywhere in plastic half-litre bottles; *it is imperative that each walker carries at least a half-litre of water — a full litre or more in hot weather.*

Nuisances

We have never been bothered by dogs but, for peace of mind, you might like to invest in an ultrasonic **dog** deterrent: contact Sunflower Books, who sell them. Any snakes you may spot slithering out of your way will probably be harmless, but **vipers** (recognisable by the distinct triangular shape of the head) *do* exist (another good reason always to wear boots and long trousers). Take care if you move a log or stone, and *always* keep a look-out near drystone walls. Outside winter you may be plagued by an encyclopaedic array of **biting insects** — just when you are panting up a mountain or tucking into lunch. You may also encounter **beehives** along some of the routes; bees are not a problem if you keep your distance.

Waymarking, grading, safety

You will encounter **waymarking** on almost all the walks, but this is not necessarily helpful. Many routes have been waymarked over the years with different colours and symbols. Only the GR (Grande Randonnée) waymarking is meticulously maintained. Local councils change PR (Petite Randonnée) routes from year to year, often *without* removing old waymarks.* Moreover, *our walks do not always follow the waymarked routes*. At the top of each walk we mention the waymarking colours *at time of writing;* although *most* PR waymarking is now yellow, this is not universal, and sometimes councils change the colours for no apparent reason. Do,

*For this reason *never* follow local footpath waymarks without the corresponding **up-to-date** IGN map or details from the tourist office (you may have to buy a book from them). You could find yourself on a dangerous path that has not been maintained for years. Beware, too, of any walks described as *sportif:* they are always potentially hazardous.

however, note these waymarking features, common to both PR and GR routes:

— A *flash* (stripe of paint) or *dot* (stipple of paint) indicates 'Route continues this way'. (The GR uses *two separate* flashes, red and white, and this must *never* be confused with a red flash on a white paint background, which is forestry marking, *not* route marking.)
— A right- or left-angled flash (or an arrow) means 'Change of direction'.
— An X means 'Wrong way'.

The walks have been **graded** for the deskbound person who nevertheless keeps reasonably fit. Our timings average 4km per hour on the flat, plus 20 minutes for every 100m/ 300ft of ascent. None of the walks ascends more than about 600m/2000ft. *Do* check your timings against ours on a short walk before tackling one of the longer hikes. Remember that these are *neat walking times;* increase the overall time by at least one-third, to allow for lunch breaks and nature-watching.

Safety depends in great part on *knowing what to expect and being properly equipped*. For this reason we urge you to read through the *whole* walk description at your leisure *before* setting out, so that you have a mental picture of each stage of the route and the landmarks. On *most* of our walks you will encounter other people — an advantage if you get into difficulty. Nevertheless, we advise you **never** to walk alone.

Maps

The **maps** in this book, adapted from the latest IGN 1:25,000 maps, have been reproduced at a scale of 1:50,000. All the latest IGN maps (the 'Top 25' Series) show many local and long-distance walks. Older IGN maps ('Série Bleue') show *only* GR routes *or none at all*. It is very difficult to plan a short or circular walk using these maps, because they do not indicate permissive routes: 'on the ground' you may come up against barbed wire or a new housing estate. If Top 25 maps are not available, you will have to seek out up-to-date walks from the local tourist office (see Bibliography).

Below is a key to the symbols on our walking maps.

motorway	spring, tank, etc	bus stop
main road	aqueduct	car parking
secondary road	church.chapel	railway station or tourist 'train'
minor road	shrine or cross	
motorable track	cemetery	castle, fort.ruins
other track	picnic tables	specified building
cart track, path, trail	pylon	quarry, mine.cave
main walk	electricity wires	windmill.stadium
alternative walk	tourist office	walkers' signpost
watercourse, pipe	mill	monument, tower
altitude	rock formation	campsite
	best views	antiquity

Walk 1: COLORADO PROVENÇAL

Distance: 7km/4.3mi; 2h10min
Grade: quite easy, with ascents/descents of about 120m/295ft overall. Good paths and tracks (but some can be wet outside summer); ample shade. Red and white GR, also private white and green waymarking; *IGN map 3242 OT*
Equipment: see page 55; also mosquito repellent. Refreshments are available at the car park.
How to get there: 🚗 to the most easterly of two car parks, just south of the D22 (Car tour 1); the turn-off is opposite the D30a to Rustrel. Paid parking with ample shade, picnic tables, route map.
Short walk: Le Sahara. 3km/2mi; 1h. Easy. Walk west along the access lane (also the GR6) to the smaller parking area, then follow white flashes or RED ARROWS ON WOODEN POSTS. This short circuit is the best part of the walk.

The whimsically-eroded cliffs, gullies and needles of the Rustrel and Roussillon ochre quarries, once exploited for natural colouring materials, today provide an endless source of fascination for the naturalist and photographer alike.

Start out in the *MAIN CAR PARK*: walk southeast on the tarred lane (GR waymarks and ▐: *CIRQUE DES BARRIES*). When the lane swings right, go straight ahead on a track, crossing the **Dòa** on stepping stones (if the river is too high, you'll have to go back 0.4km to the footbridge on the west side of the parking area; see map). Pass a *RUINED MILL* on the right (**5min**) and immediately turn right on the white-waymarked Barriès path, ignoring the GR which goes straight ahead. Five minutes later, at a Y-fork, go left to begin the Barriès circuit (ignore the sign for 'Désert Blanc' to the right). On coming to another fork immediately, keep right (WHITE ARROW). The sandy main path, looking like runny toffee, threads its way through the **Rivière de Sable** at the left of a stream, below pines and oaks.

Beyond the first of the **Cheminées de Fées** ('fairies chimneys'; eroded 'needles' of sand; ▐: *CASCADE*). The path makes a long narrow hairpin bend via this small *WATERFALL*, crosses the stream and comes back down to your outgoing route. Turn left and continue on the main path, now on the right-hand side of the stream. More fairies' chimneys rise up to the left here.

At a Y-fork keep left and, a minute later, turn left (▐: *DESERT BLANC*). Two minutes later, at another Y-fork, keep *right*. (The green-waymarked path goes left here; we

The Sahara

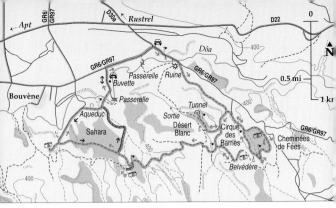

will return to it.) The white-waymarked path runs through a narrow passage into the **Désert Blanc** (**45min**), a sweep of white sand backed by white cliffs and dotted with shady pines. Ignore the sign 'Sortie' here (it leads back to the car park). Follow the ⌐ TUNNEL, immediately passing the most-photographed **Cheminée de Fée** in the Colorado and dropping down a steep narrow path to the impressive **Tunnel** — 50m/yds long and 10m/30ft high. The tunnel ends at a balcony viewpoint, so retrace your steps via the Désert Blanc and the narrow passage to the junction with the green-waymarked path (**1h**) and turn right.

Edging the southeast side of the Désert Blanc, you rise up the stony rubble of a river bed. At a Y-fork, turn left uphill. This path climbs quite steeply, then turns left and levels out amidst white cistus, pines and ferns. From the **Belvédère** (**1h10min**) there is a fine view down over the Cirque des Barriès and to Rustrel. The green-waymarked path continues east from here to the GR, but we retrace our steps back to the point where the Belvédère detour began and now turn left (⌐: SAHARA). Rising to a T-junction in two minutes, go right on a level path. Two minutes later, at a junction where 'Sortie' is ahead, go 90° left downhill for SAHARA. (This section can be *very* muddy outside sum-

mer.) Watch the waymarks on this stretch, especially as you pass through two clearings. On the far side of the second clearing, keep right for ⌐ SAHARA (or first go left to see another small cascade). Beyond a water pipe on the left, you come into the **Sahara** (**1h40min**). Make straight for the darkest red rocks seen ahead. Then climb the run of red rock on the left, to the top, for the magnificent view shown opposite — the highlights of this walk. You're surrounded by an artist's palette of yellows, oranges, mauves and burgundy reds. So intense are these reds, that in bright sunlight the foliage seems to shimmer teal blue!

To end the walk, follow the wide track (white flashes; WOODEN POSTS WITH RED ARROWS.) Walking in the *opposite* direction to the red arrows, follow the track until it goes left into a field. Here take the white-waymarked path uphill to the right. At a Y-fork, keep right to cross a stream, soon passing a lovely old AQUEDUCT on your left. Turn 90° left up a path (⌐: RETURN PARKING; **1h55min**). Descend to cross the **Dôa** on stepping stones (**2h**; or use the footbridge a short way upstream). On the far side, pass a small BUVETTE, walk up through the adjacent parking area to a tarmac lane, and turn right (GR waymarks; ⌐: BARRIES). After eight minutes turn left into the main PARKING AREA (**2h10min**).

59

Walk 2: FROM ROUSSILLON TO GORDES

Distance: 9km/5.6mi; 2h20min
Grade: very easy, except for a climb of 150m/500ft at the end. Some stony tracks underfoot; *no shade*. Red and white GR way-marking; *IGN map 3142 OT*
Equipment: see page 55. Refreshments are available at both ends of the walk.
How to get there: 🚐 to Roussillon (Car tours 1 and 2). To return, take a taxi (the taxi rank is opposite the château in Gordes), or walk back (Alternative walk).

Short walk: Roussillon's ochre quarries. 30min-1h. Easy. From the *TOURIST OFFICE* turn right and then left uphill past the *CEMETERY* (⌐: *SENTIER DES OCHRES*).
Alternative walk: Roussillon — Gordes — Roussillon. 16km/10mi; 4h10min. Grade as main walk. Retrace the GR back to the Le Buis riding school, then refer to the purple lines on the map. Although there is *no* waymarking, the route is easily followed. *Note:* Walk 3 begins and ends in Gordes.

If red is your favourite colour, then this walk will be an eyeful of delight. In spring the rose-tipped leaves of the cherry trees flutter above a carpet of scarlet poppies; in autumn rusty-red leaves mask laden vines. And above these gently-farmed fields rise two magnificently-sited hill villages. The ochre-saturated houses of Roussillon seem to 'grow' out of the quarried hillside; the steeply-stacked, honey-hued buildings of Gordes dominate the plain like an acropolis.

The walk begins on the north side of **Roussillon**, at the junction of the D105 and D169. Follow the D169 towards JOUCAS and

GORDES. Pass the D102 right to Joucas and Murs (**15min**) but, two minutes later, leave the D169: take a stony track on the right

(opposite a tarred road into a camping area). There are vineyards on the left and, beyond them, the villages of Goult, Gordes and Joucas rise from left to right. Beyond a house on the left, keep left at a Y-fork (**25min**). At the next Y-fork (**35min**), keep right. There is another fork just past here, where a track goes left and another half-left to a house. Go half-*right* here, on a footpath/bridleway, crossing the **Imergue Stream** on a concrete footbridge. On the far side of the bridge, at a fork, keep left. Two more forks follow on almost at once; keep right at both. Soon on a cart track, you pass oak tree plantations, as you head straight for Gordes, with the Petit Lubéron stretching out on your left. On reaching the curve of a tarred lane (**50min**) keep straight ahead, towards Gordes.

Pass the **Le Buis** riding school on the right and cross the D60, keeping straight ahead on a gravel track. Go straight over a tarred lane (**1h**), now following a tarmac track.

Roussillon village (far left) and main square (left). Although much smaller, Roussillon's ochre quarries (below left) are every bit as intriguing as those at the Colorado Provençal! Below: Gordes: like Roussillon, it rises above the plain shown overleaf.

The walk crosses a patchwork quilt of cultivation. Most of the fields are given over to vineyards, and an ingenious machine is used to harvest the crops! But you will also see fields of lavender against a backdrop of the Lubéron (below) and plenty of eye-catching cherry orchards.

When you come to the D2 (**1h20min**), follow it to the left and cross a bridge over the **Véroncle Stream**. Then, after 200m/yds, turn right on a stony lane (⟟: *LES GRAILLES, GORGES DE VERONCLE*). Gordes is now on the left. At a Y-fork, keep right on the main track. At the next Y-fork (almost immediately), go left uphill (⟟: *GORDES*) and pass through the holiday hamlet of **Les Grailles**. About eight minutes later, ignore a track up right; keep ahead (slightly downhill) towards Gordes, passing to the right of orchards.
Cross the D102 (**1h35min**) and

walk into the farm of **St-Eyriès**. The delightful cart track passes some bories. A tarred lane comes underfoot and takes you to the D2: turn right towards Gordes; the view on the approach is superb. At a Y-fork, go right for *LE TOURON*, climbing to the left of a huge house. As you huff and puff uphill, look back across the plain for a fine view of Roussillon. At the next Y-fork, keep right uphill. Soon a road crosses in front of you: go left downhill. But when this road again curves left downhill, turn right up the cobbled **Rue de la Fontaine** (*not* waymarked). Zigzagging up past cast-iron lamp standards and the old wash-house, this alley brings you to the *CHATEAU* in the centre of **Gordes** (**2h20min**).

Walk 3: GORDES AND THE ABBAYE DE SÉNANQUE

See map on pages 60-61
Distance: 9.5km/6mi; 2h50min
Grade: easy-moderate, with ascents/descents of 300m/1000ft overall. The paths and tracks are fairly stony, and there is little shade en route. *Faded* blue local, then red and white GR waymarking; *IGN map 3142 OT*
Equipment: see page 55. Refreshments are available only in Gordes.
How to get there: 🚗 (Car tour 2) or 🚌 to Gordes
Shorter walk: Gordes — Abbaye de Sénanque — Gordes. 5.5km/ 3.4mi; 2h20min. Grade as main walk (ascents/descents of about 250m/820ft overall). Follow the GR6 to the Abbaye de Sénanque and return the same way. Start out in the main square. Facing the Café Provençal (with the CHATEAU behind you), take the road to the left, walking past the Hotel Bas-

tide on the left. Ignore the road up right to the *gendarmerie;* cross over to the *immobilier* (estate agent), and turn left on the pavement in front of it. Watch for a FOUNTAIN with non-potable water on your right, and turn sharp right uphill on a lane just past it. Beyond a wooden gate on your right, you pick up a red and white GR waymark (5min from the château). On meeting the D177 go right but, after 200m, go left at a Y-fork (GR waymark) When you next meet the D177, bear left and follow it to a signpost, COTES DE SÉNANQUE (fine viewpoint). Now continue ahead to another sign, GARAGE 180M, on your right. On your left a sign indicates a curve in the road: the path down left to the abbey is just behind the sign.
NB: The abbey (paid admission) is closed from 12.00-15.00.

The magnificent Abbaye de Sénanque, founded by Cistercian monks in the 12th century, is the focal point for this walk. A wonderful feeling of tranquillity pervades the monastery. Pure in line, and lacking in ornamentation, most of the original buildings (and the altar) have survived to this day.

Start out in the MAIN SQUARE at **Gordes**. Facing the Café Provençal (with the CHATEAU behind you), ignore the D15 to Murs at the right of the café, take the *next* road to the right, descending past the POST OFFICE on your right. At a Y-fork, bear right, keeping the drystone walls of the CEMETERY to your left. If you look carefully, you will spot BLUE FLASHES on the wall; these waymarks are followed for the first part of the walk. Beyond the cemetery gate (**5min**), the lane eventually loses its tarred surface. When you come onto tarmac again, by a house, keep straight ahead. Just past here, at a Y-fork, go left, with magnificent drystone walls on either side. Then meet the D15 and go straight ahead, until you can turn left uphill at a sign-

post for FONTANILLE (**25min**). At the next fork, by the **Fontanille** CAMPSITE, go left. You quickly come to some LETTER-BOXES, where you turn right on a tarmac lane. The tarmac runs out and you come to a fork, where a track goes left. Take the stony path to the right — just a short-cut which rejoins the track. When the track turns off to the left, take the path straight ahead, heading due north, with fields to your right. The narrow path runs through *garrigues*, where stunted oaks provide some shade. Clumps of tiny blue grass lilies (*Aphyllanthes monspeliensis*) dot the path; they flower in May and June.
At the end of the fields, you come to a T-junction (spot height 517m; **1h05min**). There's a huge pine

63

Above: rows of lavender lead the eye to the Abbaye de Sénanque. Right: Some 3000 years of history unfold at the Village des Bories at Gordes, an outdoor museum of rural life. Bories are thought to date from the Bronze Age (while their exact origin is unknown, they resemble drystone dwellings as far afield as Ireland, Sardinia, the Balearics and Peru). Bories were inhabited until the 18th century. There is an association in Vaucluse working for the preservation and restoration of drystone structures. One of their projects is especially fascinating:

repairing the 12km-long 'Mur de la Peste', built in the 1720s between Monieux and Cabrières (Car tour 4) to halt the spread of the plague which was racing north from Marseille. At the height of the epidemic, 1000 soldiers manned this drystone wall.

tree here, offering good shade for picnicking. Turn right but, after 150m/yds, go left down a footpath (blue flashes *and red dots*). This wide stony path descends into the **Vallon de Ferrière** — a basin of lavender cultivation. Cross the valley and then climb gently to the left of the lavender, ignoring the entrance to the farm on your right. The **Sénancole Valley** opens up on the left now. At a fork, where a path goes straight ahead, keep left on a stony track and follow it southwest along the crest. Soon you have glimpses of the abbey, and you can see the Lubéron in the distance, rising from the plain. When you meet a crossing track near the hamlet of **Sénanque** (**1h 30min**), turn right downhill. The track curves left and into an open wood, another pleasant, shady picnic spot. Five minutes later you reach a crossroads with several tracks *and no waymarking*. Keep

straight ahead here on the level, motorable track. It passes to the right of a pecan grove and a large building (owned by the abbey), and takes you out to the D177 in five minutes. Cross the road and climb a path 30m/yds downhill to the left (faded *orange* flash on a rock on the right after 20 paces). In three minutes you meet a crossing path with red and white flashes (GR6/97): turn left downhill. The GR path runs just *above* the drive to the **Abbaye de Sénanque** (**1h50min**) and climbs to the D177 (**2h10min**). Bear right on the road and follow it to a sign, *COTES DE SENANQUE*. Just beyond here, turn right downhill on a stony trail, from where you can see Gordes ahead. When you next meet the D177, follow it for 200m, then fork left down a lane. Meet the main road again, in **Gordes**: turn left, then curve right, into the centre (**2h50min**).

Walk 4: CIRCUIT AROUND BUOUX

Distance: 10km/6.2mi; 2h35min
Grade: fairly easy, with ascents/descents of under 200m/650ft overall on good paths and tracks. Most of the ascents are in full sun. Variable waymarking (see text), some red and white GR waymarking; IGN *map 3242 OT*
Equipment: see page 55; water tap and restaurant at Buoux
How to get there: 🚌 to Séguin. Take the D113 east towards Buoux and turn off after 1.5km for

LES SEGUINS; park just over 1km along, past the turn-off right to FORT DE BUOUX (Car tour 2).
Short walk: Séguin — Deyme — Séguin. 5.5km/3.4mi; 1h25min. Easy, after an initial ascent of 100m/330ft. Follow the main walk for 1h, then turn left on the road (D113). In just over 1km, where the road bends to the right, go left for LES SEGUINS; your car is just past the turn-off right to the Fort de Buoux.

As you approach Séguin, a beautiful limestone edge suddenly appears on your left, on the far side of the Aigue-Brun Valley. This walk takes you along the top of the edge and then to a sunny plateau, before descending back into the valley beneath the slender tower of St-Symphorien and the ruins of the Fort de Buoux.

Start out just west of **Séguin**: continue east along the road. Where the road turns left to the inn, head right on a path. Follow the BLUE CROSS WAYMARKS (+), going downhill to the left when you come to a fork. At a second fork a minute later, again go left downhill. Now you have joined the GR9 and you cross the stream (**Aigue-Brun**; **10min**) and then a narrow watercourse.

Soon you're on a beautiful old stone-laid trail that climbs in deep zigzags (make sure, just a few minutes up, that you turn sharp left into the first of these *lacets,* where another path goes straight ahead). At first the climbing edge towers above you on the left. After an easy climb of about 15 minutes you must head up left over bare rock: you'll see two vertical GR flashes and the word BUOUX painted on a rock on your left. At the top of this small rise, where SEGUIN is painted on a rock and an arrow points back the way you came, turn left. Now a lovely earthen path takes you along the TOP OF THE CLIMBING EDGE (**30min**) through holm and holly oaks. A

farm (**Marrenon**) is hidden from view above on the right; soon you are skirting its stone walls.

Enjoy fine views down left over the Aigue-Brun Valley and, after about 15 minutes, towards the ruined Fort de Buoux almost opposite. When the GR turns off right (by a shed; **45min**), continue *straight ahead* along the cliff-edge, following blue *dot* waymarks. Lavender fields sweep away to your right, on the other side of a wall. Soon the path swings north, and the houses of Buoux come into view on the slopes ahead. A gentle descent follows, through the hamlet of **Deyme,** where tarmac comes underfoot. We soon join the D113 (**1h**). *The Short walk leaves us here and heads left downhill along this road*. Take the dirt track straight ahead, passing to the right of the popular **Auberge de la Loube** and cutting a bend off the road. When you reach the road again, turn right and pass to the left of a *gîte d'étape.* Entering **Buoux** (**1h05min**), you'll find a TAP on the right with welcome drinking water. Turn up left on a road just past the tap and

The extensive ruins of the Fort de Buoux, an oppidum inhabited from the Bronze Age until the reign of Louis XIV

just before a TELEPHONE KIOSK; you rejoin the GR9 here. Keep on tarmac, curling round to the left, to pass above a farm and then Buoux CHURCH. Then follow the road in a hairpin bend to the right, passing a SHRINE on the left. Soon, at a CHAPEL, the GR goes right on a track. Head *left* here, through broom, to skirt the chapel on a footpath.

A stony path takes you down into the **Ubac Valley** and to the Renaissance **Château de Buoux** (**1h30min**). At the château turn left on the stony access track and follow it round to left, to a surfaced road. Head straight downhill on this pretty road; tiny fields on the right, shaded by oaks, make pleasant picnic spots. You meet the D113 on a hairpin bend (**1h50min**): turn right. In under two minutes (after about 100m/ yds), turn left down a track (▪: FONTBRUME). Three minutes or so downhill, at a junction, turn left

on a track marked with the same dark blue cross waymark that you followed at the start of the walk. Step over a chain barrier barring the track to vehicles; then, just in front of the gates of the **Colonie de Vacances** owned by the city of Marseille, turn right downhill on a track. After you pass to the right of some buildings, the track turns down to the right. You cross a stream on a CON-CRETE FOOTBRIDGE (**2h**) and pick up a path. Soon there are views across the valley to the tower of **St-Symphorien**, rising above a fringe of oak leaves. The path makes a U-turn and, beyond another of the holiday camp's 'private' signs, starts to climb. *Now keep watch* for your ongoing footpath, which comes in from behind and to the left (waymarks: pale blue flashes, dark blue crosses, but *easily missed*). On coming to a Y-fork a minute along this path, keep left on the main path, hedged in by greenery. This shady footpath brings you back down to the **Aigue-Brun Stream**. You pass a grassy area on the left with a lone picnic table and soon meet the road (**2h25min**), by another signpost for the Colonie de Vacances.

Head right along the road. If you're here on a weekend, you will be treated to the breath-taking spectacle of climbers swarming over the edge like flies on a honey-pot. If you haven't already visited the **Fort de Buoux**, do so now (allow 1h extra). Or make for aptly-named 'Needle Rock' (**L'Aiguille**); it rises just beyond your PARKING PLACE (**2h35min**).

Walk 5: FORET DES CEDRES

See photograph page 16
Distance: 7.5km/4.7mi; 2h25min
Grade: easy; descent/ascent of
100m/330ft; some stony paths
and tracks. Ample shade. Blue
waymarking. *IGN map 3142 OT*
Equipment: see page 55; no
refreshments available
How to get there: 🚗 to the Forêt
des Cèdres, signposted off the
D36 (1.5km south of Bonnieux).
Paid parking at the vehicle barriers
(Car tours 2, 4).
Short walks
1 Sentier botanique. 3km/2mi;

1h08min. Grade as above. Follow
the main walk for 1h05min, then
return along the road to your car.
2 Roque des Bancs. 5km/3mi;
1h25min. Easy, level walking. Follow the Route des Crêtes for 15
minutes, until you come to a water
tank on your left. Follow the main
walk from the 1h15min-point.
3 Viewpoint. 2km/1mi; 30min.
Very easy. Follow the Route des
Crêtes *past* the Sentier botanique;
after 250m/yds turn left on a wide
path, to a fine viewpoint by ⫟ 8.
Return the same way.

C edars from the Atlas Mountains of northern Africa were
introduced on the heights of the Petit Lubéron in the mid
1800s. The trees flourished — as did the insects and mush-
rooms which arrived with them. A nature trail *(Sentier
botanique)* with information panels tells you more about the
wealth of flora and fauna on the massif.

Start out at the PARKING AREA:
follow the road behind the barrier
preventing vehicle access to the
Route des Crêtes, the narrow
tarmac road on the crest of the
Petit Lubéron. After 150m/yds
turn left (⫟: SENTIER BOTANIQUE).
Descend gently through cedars
and then *garrigues*. In spring
watch out for pockets of bright-
white star-of-Bethlehem *(Orintho-
galum umbellatum)* and the slender
stalks of the rock sainfoin
(Hedysarum saxatile), capped by a
pyramid of pale pink florets. At
the BOTTOM OF THE VALLEY
(30min), where holm oak from
these slopes used to be smouldered
into charcoal, go right uphill at the
fork. This stony path forks five
minutes later: go either way. The
two paths quickly rejoin at a BLUE
PEG, where you come to another
fork: go left uphill. In two
minutes, at a T-junction, go right,
passing ⫟6. At the next fork, seven

minutes later, climb left uphill to a
plateau. This ancient pastureland is
no longer grazed and has been
invaded by box, like so many other
upland areas we visit. At ⫟8
(55min) you come to a splendid
VIEWPOINT over the Durance
Valley, with the Montagne Ste-
Victoire visible to the left and the
Alpilles to the far right.
From here head north on a stony
track, to rejoin the **Route des
Crêtes** in 10 minutes. Turn left
and follow it to WATER TANK 41
(1h15min). Head left here, on a
footpath (BLUE FLASHES) and ignore a path off to the right almost
at once. When you come to a fork
in about seven minutes, turn right
(BLUE ARROW). Now a shady path
lined with wild flowers and junipers takes you below a limestone
edge to a BERGERIE beneath a rock
overhang **(1h40min)**. Three minutes past this shepherds' shelter go
right at a fork. Ten minutes later,
turn right on the **Route
des Crêtes** and follow it
30 minutes, back to the
CAR PARK **(2h25min)**.

Walk 6: DENTELLES DE MONTMIRAIL

Distance: 6km/3.7mi; 2h50min
Grade: moderate-strenuous, with ascents/descents of 350m/1150ft overall. Some of the descent paths are steep and stony; you must be sure-footed and agile, but the paths are not vertiginous. Little shade. Blue, then yellow PR waymarking. *IGN map 3040 ET*
Equipment: see page 55; no refreshments available beyond Gigondas
How to get there: 🚗 to the Col du Cayron (large parking area). From Gigondas (Car tour 3) follow LES FLORETS, DENTELLES DE MONTMIRAIL. When the road re- verts to track continue ahead for another 0.7km and park at the col, just over 2km from the turn-off. Or 🚐 to Gigondas and walk to the col (add 4km/1h15min return)
Short walk: Col du Cayron — Rocher du Midi — Col du Cayron. 3.5km/2.2mi; 1h40min. Moderate climb/descent of 220m/720ft, *requiring agility.* Follow the main walk for 25min, then return to the three-way signpost and head left. The distinct path climbs a bit initially, then leaves the crest and after 30 minutes descends to the Rocher du Midi (🌲). There turn right on the track back to the col.

O ne of the most exquisite walks you will ever take, *anywhere,* this magnificent hike leads you up, over and between the Dentelles and their glistening vineyards — with splendid views to Mont Ventoux.

Start out at the **Col du Cayron**: climb the signposted SENTIER D'ACCES NORD AUX DENTELLES SARRASINES. From here until you reach the Col d'Alsau, put your faith in the blue dots; the path is *very* well waymarked. At a three-way signpost (**20min**), keep straight ahead uphill (🌲: COL D'ALSAU; also blue paint marks on a rock). Five minutes later you are in the setting shown opposite (above). *(Here the Short walk returns to the signpost.)*
Turn right along the undulating ridge, rounding the **Rocher du Turc** with its 'window' (626m/2050ft, the highest point in the Dentelles). Ignore a *very difficult* path signposted back to the Rocher du Turc (**45min**); keep ahead beneath the 'window' of the **Tête Vieille.** Soon the steep descent begins (sometimes on all fours); this drops you down to the pine-scented **Col d'Alsau** (**1h05min**).
Turn left at the col but, after 50m/yds, turn left uphill (🌲: CANTON DU CLAPIS and more blue way- marks), ignoring the track right to the Tour Sarrasine. At a Y-fork almost immediately, climb steps to the right (blue *and* yellow way- marks). The climb quickly levels out, as you skirt the **Grand Montmirail** on your right. *Now you must assiduously follow sparse but crucial yellow waymarks.* Make for the 'needle' of rock seen ahead in the valley (the western edge of the **Lame du Clapis**). Just as you approach it, clamber left over bedrock (waymarked). Beyond here, bear in mind that you must cross to the far side of the valley *before* it becomes a gorge. Watch for the waymarks (near a scree) and, when the path forks, keep to the lower path. This takes you *very steeply* down to the left in hairpins — to the *only* point where you can cross the pretty rock pools of the **Ravin du Vallat de l'Aiguille** (**1h35min**).
Soon the pine-scented path heads east towards a 'sugar loaf' hill of striated rock, where you can see a chapel. Cross two streams; beyond the second you must clamber up

You climb quickly to the ridge atop the Dentelles Sarrasines (top and left), where you follow the path west past a stupendous array of jagged rocks pierced with 'windows'. From the Chapelle St-Christophe, you look out west over vineyards to Mont Ventoux.

bedrock (waymarked) and then struggle steeply up to a lane (**1h55min**). Turn right and, at a bend, climb the path up left to the beautifully-sited **Chapelle St-Christophe** (**2h05min**), a

shady spot for a break. Then return to the lane and turn right. Some 450m/yds beyond **Cassan**, at a fork (**2h20min**), go left through vineyards, back to the **Col du Cayron** (**2h50min**).

Walk 7: PONT DU GARD

See also photograph page 36
Distance: 7km/4.3mi; 2h10min
Grade: easy, with ascents/descents
of little more than 100m/330ft
overall. Some agility needed on
the 'Panorama' path and for the
descent back to the D981. Avoid
weekends and holidays, when the
Pont du Gard is swarming with
people. Yellow PR and some red
and white GR waymarking.
Limited shade. *IGN map 2941 E*
Equipment: see page 55; swimming things; refreshments
available at Vers and the Pont du
Gard
How to get there: 🚌 to Vers-
Pont-du-Gard (a detour on Car

tour 4). Vers is north of the
D981 between Uzès and Pont du
Gard (Rive Gauche). Park at the
Place de la Fontaine. Or 🚌 to
Vers
**Short walk: Rive Droite and
Rive Gauche.** 2.5km/1.6mi; 1h.
Grade as main walk. Drive to the
huge car park at Rive Gauche. Or
🚌 to Bégude de Vers-Pont-du-
Gard. Follow the main walk from
the 50min-point to the 1h20min-
point. Then walk back down
towards the left bank of the river
and follow the nature trail for as
long as you like, before returning
to the car park or bus stop.
Alternative walk: see Walk 8

Now a UNESCO World Heritage site, the Pont du Gard is a colossal work of art (see cover and page 36), to be admired from all angles, and in different lights. Plan to devote a full day to this beautiful and varied five-star walk, taking a long break on the banks of the Gardon and spending some time at the fascinating visitors' centre.

Start out in **Vers**, at the **Place de la Fontaine** (where there is a bus stop). Follow the road signposted to Uzès, passing to the right of the CHURCH and going down **Rue des Ecoles**. Keep following UZES through the **Place de l'Armistice**. Still on the D192, turn left at the **Lavoir de Font d'Izière** (5min; YELLOW WAYMARKS), pass the WINE CO-OPERATIVE on your right, and turn left on a road signposted to REMOULINS, passing an IRON CRU-

CIFIX on the left. At a T-junction, turn right in front of the CEME-TERY. Cross the RAILWAY, then immediately turn right, and after 100m/yds, turn left on a cart track through vineyards, cherry orchards and olive groves.
Cross the D981 and continue straight ahead on a tarred lane towards LA BEGUDE ST-PIERRE. Then turn left on **Chemin du Passeur**, joining the GR6. As you pass the **Hotel La Bégude St-Pierre**, turn right into its car park and continue straight off the car park on a track. On the right, the ruined **Chapelle St-Pierre** (30min), sits in a field of golden cereals and poppies.
Ignore a track to the left just past the chapel; your way becomes tarred and rises. When the lane curves left, go uphill to the right on a cart track. Ignoring turn-offs, rise to a T-junction and turn right on a level track which becomes tarred almost at once. Pass a small-

holding on the right and walk round a METAL BARRIER, to continue on the lane. When you reach a barrage of SIGNPOSTS (**45min**), *keep straight ahead on the lane* ([■]: PONT DU GARD 0,8KM). ('Pont du Gard' is also signposted half-right here via the GR; this is the return route.)

When the tarmac ends, descend ahead to a walkway (**50min**): the **Pont du Gard** is to your right. Follow the paved path and cross the bridge. On the far side, take steps up to the right, to a fine view of the river and bridge. At the top of the steps, turn right for PANO-RAMA (**55min**), now following *GR waymarks*. Beyond the VIEW-POINT (just a couple of minutes up), continue on this path which zigzags back down to the river. Meeting the lane on the south side of the bridge, turn right, walk below one of the arches and after 100m/yds, turn back sharp right to cross back to the *rive gauche* (left bank). Here go straight ahead up steps ([■]: GR6/63, PR41). From here on the maze of paths through the *garrigues* can be confusing, so keep a close eye on the yellow and red and white waymarks; *you should always be on a strong, clear, waymarked path.* But first make a short detour left, to the left bank's PANORAMA (**1h20min**).

The route goes through a beautiful wood of holly and holm oak, where the yellow and red fruits of the strawberry tree and pink cistus shine against the dark foliage. Soon remains of the old aqueduct begin appearing on the left. When you come back to the SIGNPOSTS first encountered at the 45min-point (**1h30min**), cross straight over the lane ([■]: VERS). There are even more substantial remains on this stretch. At a crossing with a lane on the left and a track to the right, go straight ahead up a steep dirt path. There is

Substantial remains of the old aqueduct south of the D981

a beautiful setting not far along, with rocks placed in a circle beneath a huge holm oak on the right — a perfect picnic spot. Soon you descend have to descend an embankment, to a track just above the D981 — a steep, awkward drop of about 4m/12ft. Walk 100m/yds to the left on the track, to a small roundabout. Go right, cross the D981 *carefully*, then go straight ahead on a road signposted CARRIERES DE VERS-EST. Cross the RAILWAY (**1h50min**) and immediately turn right up a motorable gravel track. At the top of the rise, make a U-turn to the left ([■]: FONTAINE MENESTIERE), then keep left at a Y-fork. The arches and buttresses of the ruined aqueduct are still beside you. Keep left at two more Y-forks and then turn left at a T-junction; *watch the yellow waymarks on this stretch!* Finally the aqueduct ends and you come onto a motorable track: keep straight ahead. Just as this track becomes tarred (by a FIRE HYDRANT on the left), turn left on a pretty woodland path. It comes down to the D227 at the **Fontaine de Misserand**. Turn right on the road, then take the first right uphill (RUE DU LAVOIR). Keep straight ahead past any turn-offs. At a T-junction go left downhill (**Chemin des Crozes**). Continue to the CHURCH and the **Place de la Fontaine** (**2h20min**).

Walk 8: GORGES DU GARDON

Distance: 11km/6.8mi; 3h05min
Grade: easy, level walking, but the bedrock sections can be very slippery when wet. The short, steep ascent to the Chapelle St-Vérédème demands a head for heights. Yellow PR waymarks. *IGN map 2941 O*
Equipment: see page 55; optional bathing things; a **strong torch** is mandatory, if you want to explore La Baume, a cave/tunnel. Refreshments available at Collias
How to get there: 🚌 to Collias (Car tour 5); park at the FOYER CULTUREL on the D3 in the village.
Alternative walks
1 **Return via Les Condamines.** 12.5km/7.8mi; 4h15min. Moderate, with ascents/descents of about 150m/490ft, requiring agility. Virtually *no shade*. If you want to make the walk circular, return to the 1h20min-point and climb the

steep path and then a *very* steep escarpment (RED DOTS, YELLOW FLASHES). Beyond a vineyard on the right, you meet a cart track (40min). Turn left and, after 25m/yds, at the **Les Condamines** signpost, follow 🠖: COLLIAS 5.7KM. 300m/yds further on, at a Y-fork, ignore signposting left to Collias; keep *right* following *sparse* GR waymarks (🠖: MENUDE; GR6/63). This stony track leads back to Collias. The views north over the Alzon Valley are fine (and you can also divert right to some viewpoints over the Gardon), but in heat the route is soul-destroying.
2 **Collias — Pont du Gard.** (6.5km/4mi; 2h15min). This walk is part of a network of hikes in the Gardon. You could, for instance, link up with Walk 7. A good route map showing signposting is available from the local tourist offices.

T his splendid walk is best reserved for a quiet weekday out of season, to ensure absolute tranquillity. The hundreds of caves along the little gorge were inhabited in paleolithic times; today much of the riverbank is a nature reserve, where fish and beavers thrive. The once-cultivated fields are overgrown with wild flowers, a magnet for butterflies.

Start out at the FOYER CULTUREL in **Collias**: walk south to the river and descend the steps just before the bridge (🠖: LA BAUME). At the bottom of the steps, take the road ahead and continue on track past a kayaking centre. Beyond a restaurant, you're on a wide shady track beside the **Gardon**. Rock walls rise on your right, while the far bank is backed by gentle wooded hills. Soon the way narrows to a riverside path. You *may* come to a point (after about **20min**) where the path has been diverted away from the river for a short stretch to protect the beavers' habitat; if so, *watch out* for the tree stumps in the path.)
After passing a nature reserve sign asking you to keep to the main

path, you come to the most beautiful stretch, as you continue over bedrock. The river is utterly placid, limpid, and brimming with surprisingly large fish. Then the path moves inland through tall golden grasses full of wild flowers, where legumes and sugar cane testify to cultivation in centuries past.
Some rapids are passed and the path crosses a short ledge below a huge boulder, the **Rocher Tombé** (**45min**) before running alongside the river again. Notice the pink and white marble-like bedrock underfoot.
Finally you come to another signpost indicating a path climbing to the right (🠖: LES CONDAMINES; **1h20min**). *(This is*

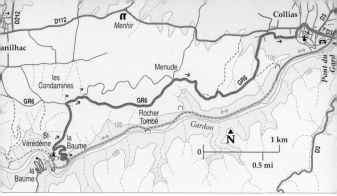

the easiest ascent for the Alternative walk.) Ahead is a dam, and the ruins of **La Baume** on the far bank. Unless you have a head for heights, this is a good place to end the walk with a picnic, while you watch the kayakers by the dam. The main walk continues past a WATERMILL (**1h25min**), turns north and then zigzags uphill (partially on steps) to the ruined **Chapelle St-Vérédème** (**1h35min**). A monk's cell is to the left of the chapel and a narrow, exposed, cliff-edge path runs to the right of it. Follow this short path through an iron gate, to **La Baume**, an enormous cave-tunnel. *Don't go more than a few steps into this cave/tunnel unless you have a very good torch;* it is enormous, pitch black (because it curves), and can be extremely frightening. On the other hand, if you *do* have a good torch and you are keen to do Alternative walk 1, you can walk *through* this cave/tunnel and then

follow a short path which leads to the steep Condamines ascent. The best way to end the walk is to retrace your steps along the riverbank to **Collias** (**3h05min**).

Below: view over the Gardon from the Chapelle St-Vérédème; bottom: the watermill and dam at La Baume

Walk 9: CIRCUIT TO THE CASCADES DU SAUTADET

la Roque-sur-Cèze
Cèze
D980
Cascades du Sautadet
Forêt Communale de la Roque
N
0   1 km
0.5 mi
D166
Rochers de Descattes
Darboussas
D143
D143

shooting in the woods above La Roque. Some stony tracks, but mostly pleasant paths underfoot. *No waymarking. IGN map 2940 OT* **Equipment:** see page 55; bathing things. Refreshments at La Roque **How to get there:** 🚌 to La Roque-sur-Cèze (optional detour on Car tours 4, 5, 6). From Remoulins take the N86 north. Just past Bagnols-sur-Cèze, turn left on the D980 for BARJAC and after about 9km turn left again for LA ROQUE. Cross the old bridge (one-way system; traffic light) and turn down right into the large shaded parking area.

Distance: 6,5km/4mi; 2h30min
Grade: quite easy, with an ascent/descent of 175m/575ft. Avoid the walk on Tue/Sat/Sun/ holidays, when there is boar-

Short walk/picnic suggestion: Cascades du Sautadet. 40min. Easy. From the car park, follow the lane on the west side of the river to the waterfalls and back.

This woodland walk, with an optional swim at the end, is ideal for a warm day. Much of the route is in deep shade, on leaf-soft, sunken footpaths, before emerging in vineyards. The 13th-century arched bridge at La Roque is a beauty, and the village worth a visit. But without doubt it is the unique maze of waterfalls the Cèze has cut into the limestone rock at the Cascades du Sautadet that will stay in your memory.

Start the walk at the PARKING AREA below **La Roque:** follow the road up into the village. Curl left uphill in front of the CHURCH on the **Grande Rue**, pass a tiny square on the left, and then keep straight ahead up a stone-laid road (still the **Grande Rue**). Pass the **Mairie** on the left (**9min**), then head left above it on the **Chemin de Bellefeuille**, passing a few houses. At a three-way fork (where the tar runs out; **15min**), take the middle track. Six minutes later, ignore a track off left. Two minutes further on, you come to a clear junction of tracks where there is a sign about boar-hunting (SANGLIERS). Turn left here, enjoying a pleasant view northwest over the Cèze Valley. One minute after passing a vineyard on the left,

at a Y-fork, keep left, perhaps passing an improvised 'barbecue' and table on the left immediately. The way continues through a thick *maquis* of junipers, holm oaks, strawberry trees, pines, and bright pink-flowering cistus. Soon bedrock comes underfoot — an especially attractive section. Beyond a rise (**50min**), a lovely woodland trail with moss underfoot undulates to the CREST of the **Rochers de Descattes** (**55min**). Here the main trail turns 90° left, but you must *turn off right* on a strong path. (The main trail continues along the crest, with fine views after 10-15 minutes.) Just 10m/yds downhill, your path curls left and you can see a LARGE CAIRN just below. Beyond the cairn, the path (sometimes sunken) descends

74

gently southeast through a dense canopy of oaks.

When you come to a CLEARING WITH A HUGE OAK in the centre, ignore the track ahead. Turn 90° left on a level path, also sunken, through shady mixed woodland. You may spot some holes underfoot, where wild boar have been rooting. Ignore all side paths as you traverse east, eventually through a patch of maritime pines. The path emerges on a track in front of a VINEYARD (**1h30min**), with a fine view across the Cèze Valley and back up to the Rochers de Descattes. Follow this cart track to the right and descend straight ahead between vineyards, ignoring tracks left and right. You will pass a farm on the left (with nasty and possibly *unchained* dogs) and immediately come to the D166. Opposite is a lane to a camp site, but take the track just at the left of this lane. At the Y-fork which comes up in a minute, go left downhill on a rocky path (ignoring a track which comes in from the right). Three minutes later, at a T-junction with a track, turn left downhill (a gated entrance is to the right). Ignore a track coming in from the left behind you four

minutes later. Two minutes after that, join a lane and keep left, between vineyards lined with oaks and acacias.

Just 10m/yds *before* joining the D166 again (**1h50min**), turn 90° right on a cart track between vineyards, making for a stone farm building ahead, behind a cypress tree. Two parallel cart tracks run towards this building; keep to the left-hand one. After passing to the left of the building, curl left on the track, rounding the vineyard. After a good 100m/yds (where the track curls half-left), take a *good, clear* path down right through trees (there are some minor, overgrown paths down right before this one.) In two minutes you're on the shingle beach beside the **river Cèze** (**2h**), where you turn left upstream alongside the **Cascades du Sautadet**. (But if you plan to swim, do so now: it's forbidden at the falls.) From here allow at least 30 minutes to walk back to your car. There's a good, shady path at the left of the falls (with pine-shaded picnic spots), but boulder-hopping is a must! At the top end of the falls, turn left to a lane and follow it back to the PARKING AREA below **La Roque** (**2h30min**).

Cascades du Sautadet: Legend has it that Hannibal's daughter drowned here, while trying to cross the river on her elephant...

Walk 10: GORGES DE L'ARDECHE

Distance: about 5km/3mi; 2h
Grade: fairly easy, but you must be sure-footed. *This walk should only be attempted after a period of settled dry weather; it is **dangerous** in wet conditions.* If there has been heavy rain, the bedrock beside the gorge will take a couple of days to dry. Otherwise it can be difficult just to stand upright, and there are several awkward rock steps and ledges en route. Yellow and white waymarking, *which must be followed assiduously.* IGN map 2939 OT
Equipment: see page 55; refreshments at Sauze, Les Grottes
How to get there: 🚌 (optional detour on Car tours 4-7) to one of three starting points (see below)

We've dipped (almost literally) into this walk three times and found it surprisingly tiring. Perhaps we've been unlucky, with wet conditions and impassable fords. But *do* be prepared to make slower progress than you might expect of a riverside stroll! Much of the walk is over bedrock — as slippery as ice in wet conditions, and there are a few quite awkward rock ledges to scramble over.

Rather than give precise route descriptions and timings, we suggest three ways to start the walk, and how far you might reasonably hope to get. The map shows only a small section of the gorge; if you want to try to reach the Cirque de la Madelaine, the most dramatic meander in the gorge, buy the IGN map on site. All the starting points are off the main tourist road between Vallon Pont d'Arc and St-Just (D290) — easily reached as a detour during Car tours 4, 5 or 6.

1 **Start out** at the CAMP SITE at **Sauze** (paid parking). This is the most popular starting point, so will be *very* crowded on weekends and holidays. It is signposted off the D290 about 2km northwest of St-Martin d'Ardèche. A track leads to a sign, GORGES DE L'ARDECHE — RESERVE NATURELLE, where you turn down to the river. The most awkward points, if you begin here, are encountered below the **Ranc Pointu** viewpoint, where the rock steps demand sure-footedness and caution, and at **Le Détroit**, where there is another awkward ledge to

negotiate. From this starting point you might walk to the CAMP SITE **Les Grottes** and back (**2h30min**).
2 **Start out** 200m east of the **Ranc Pointu** viewpoint on the D290 (ample parking beside the road). From here a path descends 100m/330ft into a side-valley and then the main gorge (15min). Advantages: fewer people, free parking, avoids the steps at Ranc Pointu. Disadvantages: The final descent down a 4m/12ft-high ledge is via iron rungs bolted into the rock, and you still encounter the awkward ledge at **Le Détroit**.

76

When you reach the CAMP SITE of **Les Grottes** (**30min**) — and 'grotty' it is, too, with all the ghetto blasters and unclad bodies sprawled about — you're likely to find it closed off with tape. Just ignore the tapes and plough right through, averting your eyes. Continue as long as you like along the gorge — perhaps to the **Rapide de la Cadière** and back (**2h**).

3 **Start out** at the BUVETTE at **Les Grottes**. This is signposted off the D290 opposite the **Grotte de St-Marcel** and **Sentier botanique**, some 4km west of the Ranc Pointu viewpoint (1.5km down a dirt track). From here it's about 5km/3mi; 2h to the Cirque de la Madelaine, so you might make it! Then again, like us, you might find the ford 1.5km south of the *cirque* impassable! (Hint: the *Sentier botanique* at St-Marcel is enjoyable; allow 1h30min.)

Autumn brings a lovely glow to the gorges, especially late in the afternoon.

Walk 11: ST-MICHEL-DE-FRIGOLET AND BARBENTANE

Distance: 9km/5.6mi; 2h35min
Grade: easy, with ascents/descents of about 100m/330ft overall. Only the yellow PR waymarking between the abbey and Barbentane is *reliable*. It helps to have a good sense of direction, as there are many woodland tracks. *IGN map 3042 O*
Equipment: see page 55; refreshments available at the abbey (pm only) or Barbentane

How to get there: 🚌 to the **Draille du Mas de la Dame**, a motorable track running southeast off the D35e, 2.2km north of the Abbey of Frigolet (Car tour 5). Large shaded parking area just at the start of this track.
Short walk: St-Michel-de-Frigolet (4.2km/2.6mi; 1h10min). Easy. Follow the main walk to the 1h08min-point, then keep straight ahead, back to your car.

The plain below La Montagnette, a pocket-sized mountain astride the Rhône, is the setting for a delightful walk through woodlands and beside flower-filled olive groves, with the option of a visit to the abbey of St-Michel-de-Frigolet and the charming village of Barbentane with its exquisite château.

Start out at the PARKING AREA by heading southeast on the stony track that passes *between* a WELL on the left and an SHRINE on the right. Just before this track joins the D35e, take a wide path on the left. After passing to the right of a large BUILDING FOUNDATION IN RUINS (**5min**), turn left at a T-junction. After 30m/yds, go right uphill on another path in the **Bois de Barbentane** — the prettiest woodland path on the walk, almost jungle-like in places. After passing through a clearing and going round a wire barrier, cross the scruffy forestry works area, bearing right on a forestry track. From now on, *just keep to the left of the D35e,* whether on track or path. Go through a TALL HEDGE OF CYPRESSES and continue 250m/yds to the abbey of **St-Michel-de-Frigolet** (**30min**). Whether or not the 19th-century buildings are to your taste, the church is open daily and houses the original abbey, the 11th-century chapel of **N-D-du-Bon-Remède**, with beautiful gilt panelling. There is also a café open in the afternoons.

After your visit, return to the CYPRESS HEDGE and turn right in front of it. At the end of the hedge, ignore two paths to the left, but take the third, wider, rising path half-left. *Just 75 paces from the cypresses,* turn right down a clear but narrow path into a gully. A pretty path through *maquis* takes you out of the gully, then dips again — to the hairpin bend of a track (**40min**). Turn right, beginning to round the **Mont de la Mère**. The next fork, 150m/yds further on, is an IMPORTANT JUNCTION: go left.

The track curls right and downhill, with the stony hillock of Mont de la Mère still beside you on the left. At the next, Y-fork, keep right, downhill, with an OLIVE GROVE down to the right. Two minutes later step around a CHAIN BARRIER (where a track comes in from the right, behind you). The track now curls right in front of an enclosure, where you should see lamas as well as donkeys and horses. Pass a house on the left and then the **Mas de la Dame** on the right (**55min**). You are now walking on the **Draille du Mas de la Dame**, off which you parked. After 900m/0.6mi (**1h08min**), watch for the back of a road sign on your left (it *may* bear a yellow 'X'): turn

78

St-Michel-de-Frigolet

right here, then right again. *(But for the Short walk, keep straight on.)* Beyond an olive grove on the left you come to another *mas* (with a fenced-in dog) and a junction: go left here, ignoring tracks to the right and straight ahead. Pass a second entrance to the same estate (on the left) and ignore a track to the right just opposite it. But at the next, Y-fork, go right. After 100m/yds, at a T-junction, go left. Pass a shed in a pretty grassy area on the right and come to cross-roads at a clearing, with POWER LINES overhead. Keep straight ahead, downhill. When a track comes in from the left, behind you, keep right downhill. Walk to the left of a cherry orchard and under more power lines. Just before an IRON CROSS (**Croix de Chaulet; 1h 30min**), turn right on a country lane. Over to the left, across fields, you can see the Château de Barbentane on a slight, wooded rise. Some 400m/yds along turn left on a cart track (opposite FIRE TRACK 7). This route is a delight of colourful hedgerows and olive groves. Just beyond the **Mas de Bassette** (**1h50min**) go straight ahead on a tarred road, passing an IRON CROSS atop a mound on the right. Rise to a T-junction and turn left on the **Chemin Moulin de Brétoule** through a pleasant modern housing estate. Keep on this road past a FOOTBALL PITCH (behind cypresses on the left) and then an olive grove (also on the left). At another T-junction, with an old WINDMILL up to the right

(**1h55min**), turn left and walk to the main road. Cross over into **Barbentane** CAR PARK (with a walkers' information panel). Walk to the right of the car park, then take the chained-off path between another information panel on the left and a house on the right. Stay on this main path which rises and widens to a track. Ignore all turn-offs until you come to a major fork (**2h10min**), where you keep right uphill. As you pass under POWER LINES (**2h23min**), keep straight ahead, ignoring a track to the right and another running downhill to the left. You can now see a farm on the D35e over to the left. So as not to overshoot your goal, take the *next* track off left (it *may* bear a blue waymark), and make your way over to the D35e. Turn right on the road for the short distance back to the **Draille du Mas de la Dame** (**2h35min**).

Walk 12: ST-REMY AND LES BAUX-DE-PROVENCE

See also photographs on pages 27, 28-29

Distance: 15km/9.3mi; 4h15min
Grade: moderate, with ascents/descents of 250m/820ft overall. The walk mostly follows tracks which are stony underfoot. *Not recommended in hot weather, as there is almost no shade. Yellow PR waymarking and red and white GR waymarking, but some sections are not waymarked. IGN map 3042 O*
Equipment: see page 55. Refreshments available at Les Baux, halfway through the walk
How to get there: 🚌 to the large parking area at the lake (Barrage des Peiroou) near St-Rémy. Follow the D5 south out of St-Rémy (Car tour 5). Note the km reading when you pass the tourist office (on your right); 0.5km further on, turn right for LE BARRAGE; the parking area is 2km further on. Or 🚐 to Les Baux and do the circuit from there (the 1h45min-point in the walk). Also accessible by 🚐 to St-Rémy, but you will have to add an extra 6km/1h45min from there to the lake and back.

Short walks

1   St-Rémy — Les Baux. 6km/3.7mi; 2h. Grade as main walk, but the climb is under 150m/500ft. Follow the main walk to Les Baux and from there catch a bus back to St-Rémy (add up to 3km/45min to walk on to your car) or take a taxi back to the lake (the taxi rank is by the bus stop in Les Baux).

2   Les Baux — St-Rémy. 8km/5mi; 2h15min. Easy. Use the notes for Car tour 5, page 28, to park at the viewing table near Les Baux. Follow the walk from the 2h45min-point to the end, then walk on from the lake to the D5 and follow it to the tourist office in St-Rémy, where they can advise on buses or call a taxi to take you back to your car. (If you take a bus back to Les Baux, allow another 45min to walk back to your car.) If you pre-arrange for a taxi to meet you at the lake, reckon on 5.5km/3.4mi; 1h30min.

Alternative route: Piste des Lombards. This PR-waymarked route is highlighted in purple on the map.

This delightful ridge walk is probably the most popular in the Alpilles, and deservedly so: it's not too long or too steep, and it leads from a gorgeous lake to one of the most famous beauty spots in France, the magnificently-sited citadel of Les Baux, shown on pages 28-29. Les Antiques and Glanum are close to the lake where the walk begins and ends, so plan to spend the whole day in this area.

Start out at the lake, the **Barrage des Peiroou**, much favoured by picnickers and anglers. Ignore the track closest to the lake. Locate the red and white flashes of the GR6 (**ᵀ**: SENTIER GR6) and follow the GR uphill through pines on an earthen track. In two minutes cross the road to the lake and take the stony track opposite. After 12 minutes, a PR path waymarked in yellow goes off to the left: ignore it; follow the track round to the right, to a tarred area with a CISTERN (**15min**). Continue straight ahead along the tar, ignoring a track descending to the right. Looking left now, you'll see the huge ORTF relay equipment on the bluff of La Caume.
Ignore a path to the right and then two tracks going off to the left (not shown on the map); keep on

the main track, which bends sharply to the right. You enjoy good views to the north, before the track turns southwards again. At this point (**30min**; spot height 266m) the main track continues ahead, but we fork right uphill on a footpath with both red and white GR waymarks and yellow PR waymarks. (This footpath gives super views of the north from a crest. If you prefer to avoid the climb, or if a *mistral* is blowing, stay on the track and fork right when you come to a T-junction almost at once.) So far the ascent has been imperceptible, but now we *do* climb. In about six minutes we reach the top with its fine views and gale-force winds. Five minutes later we're back down on the main track. Continue southwest along the main track now, ignoring a minor cart track going off to the right. Two minutes along ignore a track (A143) coming in from the left and then a track off right to the fire watchtower (**Tour de Guet**); continue straight ahead.
Now we are going to part company with the GR and take a much more attractive path. This path is *not waymarked*, so follow the notes carefully. Five minutes past the track up to the watchtower (**55min**) the main track describes a deep U-bend, and you come to a junction of paths and tracks: a path comes down from the watchtower on the right, and another path goes out left to a

View from the Table d'Orientation across the Val d'Enfer to Les Baux triangulation point. Leave the main track here (it is the return route): take the track to the left of the main track, but to the right of the path to the triangulation point. You are walking parallel with the main track, but descending. After about 100m/yds downhill, turn left on another track — the first one you come to. Now you're heading in the direction of the triangulation point, and soon the track becomes a lovely grassy footpath. Not far along, a path comes down from the triangulation point and joins you from the left. After descending for about 15 minutes meet a wide stony crossing path (**1h15min**) and turn left; you may see some fluorescent orange waymarks underfoot. In two minutes go round a chain barrier, then meet another track and turn left (above a house with an *unchained* dog). Pass two houses on the right and immediately come to a tarred junction. Turn right, gradually descending. (An alternative route, waymarked in yellow, comes in from the left after 600m/yds; see purple lines on the map.) After 650m/yds you meet the D27a (**1h30min**). Now you have to follow this road just over 1.5km uphill to **Les Baux**, but all along the road there are fine views to the bauxite mines and Les Baux rising on the cliffs. Continue uphill to the parking area and walk past the PARKING ATTENDANT'S STONE KIOSK (**2h**; BUS STOP, TAXI RANK). Up on your left, before you come to entrance to the village, is

The Barrage des Peiroou (top) and flowering fields below the crests

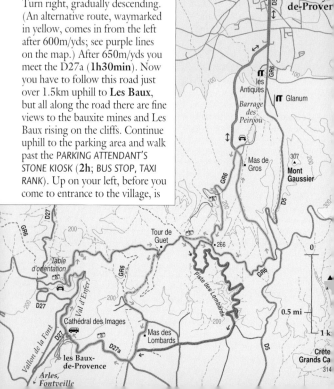

a shop selling snacks and drinks — a great pit stop on a hot day, especially if you don't want to join the midday crowds at the citadel. From the shop walk back downhill past the parking attendant's kiosk and, when you are back on the D27a, turn left downhill towards FONTVIEILLE and ARLES. When you reach the D27 go right, ignoring the left turn for Fontvieille and Arles. Soon you pass the **Cathédral des Images** and yet more mines. Just beyond the sign denoting the EXIT FROM LES BAUX (**2h20min**), turn right on a track and walk to the right of a chain barrier (prohibiting vehicles). After climbing for less than 15 minutes, come to a T-junction with a stony track and turn left, still climbing (here you join a PR route waymarked in yellow). Three minutes uphill you round a bend and have a most magnificent view over to the left, across the Val d'Enfer and to Les Baux: the old mines are in foreground on other side of valley, with the village and the citadel behind them. The gentle Vallon de la Font spreads out to the right of the citadel. Some 25 minutes off the D27 meet a tarmac road and cross straight over: climb the steep path opposite to the **Table d'Orientation** (viewing table; **2h45min**). Unless it is very hazy, you will have good views of the Camargue and the Rhône Valley, the Lubéron and Mont Ventoux. *(Short walk 2 starts here.)* From the *table d'orientation* walk down the wide track. Join the tarmac road but, where it swings right, back towards Les Baux, go straight ahead on a tarmac lane, behind a chain barrier. Stalwart yellow mullein blooms here in summer. Five minutes along, at a Y-fork, ignore the concreted fire point up to the right; keep left along the track. Ten minutes later

ignore the overgrown track on the right; keep left on the main track (both yellow PR and red and white GR waymarks). Half an hour from the *table d'orientation* (**3h15min**) you rejoin your outgoing route, when you round the U-bend below the fire watchtower. Five minutes later pass the track up to the watchtower and two minutes after that the path you descended from the ridge-top viewpoint; keep right along the track here. Three minutes later, where a fainter track goes downhill to the right, keep left on a level track. It curls around to offer a superb view of the Alpilles and La Caume. Three minutes later pass the path you climbed to the ridge-top viewpoint, now on your left. Follow the track in a curve to the right. You come to a ROCK CUTTING (spot height 266m; if you turn down left here, you can descend along your outgoing route, saving about 15-20 minutes). The main walk continues past the cutting. Looking down left through the trees, soon you will spot the lake where you set out, with the spire of St-Rémy's church behind it. Ignore any grassy tracks downhill either side of the main track. The downhill track you want comes up about 20 minutes past the cutting (**3h55min**) — only about 150m/yds short of the D5. Look ahead through the pines on the left, and you'll see large white arrows pointing you downhill (along FIRE ROUTE A38; fire route A7, which you have been following, now continues ahead to the D5). Turn left downhill on this pine-shaded but stony track. On reaching the tarmac road to the lake, turn right downhill to the **Barrage des Peiroou** (**4h15min**).

Walk 13: LE DESTET AND AUREILLE

Distance: 7.5km/4.7mi; 2h30min
Grade: easy, with ascent/descent of about 100m/330ft overall, but there is *no shade.* Some blue dots, some red and white GR waymarking. *IGN map 3043 E*
Equipment: see page 55; refreshments available at Aureille
How to get there: 🚐 to Le Destet (southeast of St-Rémy, Car tour 5). From the junction of the D78 and D24 drive south towards Mouriès along the D24 and after 200m turn left on the first track you come to (one of the signposts here reads VALLEE DES BAUX). Continue uphill for about 0.8km and park off the side of the track when you are level with the far end of

the moto-cross circuit.
Short walk: Vaudoret. 4.5km/ 2.8mi; 1h35min. Easy, with minimal ascents. Follow the main walk for 40min, then turn right downhill. Pick up the notes again after the 1h35min-point.
Alternative walk: Le Destet — Tour des Opies — Le Destet. 15km/9.4mi; 5h20min. Strenuous and long, with an overall ascent/ descent of 450m/1475ft. Follow this walk to Aureille (1h05min), then make your way to the cemetery below the château. Do Walk 14, then return to Aureille for some refreshments. When you are ready to leave, pick up this walk again at the 1h05min-point.

Silvery leaves glisten beneath a porcelain-blue sky, and the air shimmers with heat, as you walk to the pretty village of Aureille and then through olive groves typical of the Alpilles. Choose a cool day between October and May for this countryside ramble *in full sun.*

Start out by trudging east along the track from the *MOTO-CROSS CIRCUIT* where you parked. Ignore the tracks off right to the farm of Vaudoret (**5min, 15min**). We'll delve into the Vaudoret olive groves later in the walk. At the next, three-way junction (under **20min**) take the middle track or the one on the left (they rejoin); the track on the right is our return route. Four minutes later, ignore a track left uphill but, three minutes further on, at a Y-fork, *do* go left (and ignore a path off to the right a minute uphill). This track skirts to the right of a cultivated field, then brushes up against the cliffs we have been following since starting out. Notice the turpentine trees (*Pistacia terebinthus*), with

their shiny leaves and autumn clusters of reddish-brown fruits. You eventually approach a couple of BUILDINGS on the left (**35min**). Continue past them on a very overgrown track. It loops away from the cliff wall and skirts a field full of thistles. Keep to the left-hand side of the field; a stream is on your left. On meeting a stronger crossing track, under four minutes past the buildings, turn left, crossing the STREAM. A minute later (**40min**), ignore a strong track coming in from the left; keep straight ahead. But notice, almost immediately, the good track down right into the olive groves — your return route. *(The Short walk goes right here.)* Now ignore a track off to the

right; continue ahead over a rushing WATERCOURSE. Keep ahead past another track off right, soon coming to a crest with a fine view ahead to Aureille, crowned by its château. A beautiful rounded mountain with a tower rises behind the village: Les Opies — the highest point in the Alpilles (Alternative walk). Tar comes underfoot at a housing estate, where you join the GR6. When you come to a Y-fork, bear right on **Rue du Batiment**. Turn right to cross the pretty stream, and then go left towards the clock tower in **Aureille** (**1h05min**); a bar/café is just opposite. Have a look at the unusual church before you leave Aureille.

Leave Aureille the way you came in (Rue du Batiment) and, at a Y-fork, keep right with the GR6 on the **Chemin de St-Jean**. When the tar ends (and the GR turns up right), note the time. Under 10 minutes later you will cross the rushing watercourse again. Just beyond it is your turn-off (left) into the **Vaudoret** olive groves (**1h35min**).

Down in the heart of the groves, you meet a T-junction after 15 minutes: turn right into a quintessential Alpilles setting, with olive groves in the foreground and a backdrop of limestone cliffs. As the track curls round to the right, back towards the cliffs, the way is brighted by bright pinky-purple cranesbill (*Geranium tuberosum*) and Scottish thistles.

When you rejoin your outgoing route at the three-way fork (**2h20min**), turn left, back to your car near the MOTO-CROSS CIRCUIT (**2h30min**).

Near Le Destet (top) and the Vaudoret olive groves (above).

Below: Aureille's church and view to Aureille from a shrine west of the village: the ruined château can be seen just to the right of the shrine, and the Tour des Opies (Walk 14) on the mountaintop just above the château.

Walk 14: TOUR DES OPIES

Map and photos pages 84-85
Distance: 7.5km/4.7mi; 2h50min
Grade: moderate ascent of 350m/
1150ft, but you must be sure-
footed and agile. Do not attempt
the summit on windy days. Although the path is well used, be
prepared to push through prickly
broom. Little shade. GR waymarking at the start; vivid green to
the pass; *no* waymarking to the
summit. *IGN map 3043 E*
Equipment: see page 55; suitable
clothing for dense undergrowth;
walking stick(s). Refreshments
available at Aureille
How to get there: 🚌 to Aureille,
(on the D25a, 12km from Le Destet; detour on Car tour 5). Park at
the cemetery below the village.

One of our favourite hikes, this gorgeous, varied walk
leads through dense *maquis,* with a huge variety of wild
flowers, and a fairy-tale wood, before struggling up to a
restored Saracen tower with panoramic views.

Start out at the CEMETERY in
Aureille. Follow the track heading
east towards the tower atop the
Opies; a GR waymark is on a tree
on your right. At a first fork, keep
right on the main track. Bear left
at a second fork (**5min**; GREEN
ARROW), leaving the GR. Keep to
the left of an ANIMAL ENCLOSURE
WITH TREES, ignoring a track off to
the left. The stony track swings
round to the right and narrows
(**25min**). (At this point, ignore a
path to the left.) Be prepared now
to push your way through tall
thickets of pricky broom; the path
itself is very clear underfoot.
At a Y-fork (**45min**) keep right
(GREEN WAYMARK on a stone) and
rise through the welcome shade of
a dense woodland bower.
On reaching the PASS below the
tower (**1h05min**; HUGE CAIRN),
you enjoy a superb view north to
the Vallon de Valdelègue; the
tower is up to your right. From
here take the path running sharply
up to the right; it soon frays out
into many strands (avoid minor
short-cut paths to the left), but
your goal is obvious. The path
rounds the southwest side of the
summit, comes to another huge
CAIRN, then heads hard left. Just
before reaching the METAL POLE
below the tower, turn up *right* for
the easiest final scramble. From
the **Tour des Opies (1h30min)**
the views are tremendous, taking
in Aureille far below, the Alpilles,
La Caume with its transmitter, the
Etang de Berre and Mediterranean
in the south, and — conditions
permitting — Ste-Victoire to the
east and even Mont Ventoux to
the north!
Return the same way to **Aureille**
(**2h45min**).

*View to Aureille and La Caume, not
far below the tower (top), and the
flower-filled summit ascent path*

Walk 15: DIGUE A LA MER

Distance: 7.5km/4.7mi; 2h15min
Grade: easy, level walk along stony tracks. But flat walks along blinding-white tracks where there is no shade can be surprisingly tiring. We would not recommend any walks longer than 2-3 hours in the Camargue. Rent a bicycle instead! *No waymarking. IGN map 2944 E.*
Equipment: see page 55; trainers will suffice. *Adequate sun protection is mandatory; the cool breeze is deceptive, and sunstroke is a real possibility.* If you take a picnic, remember that any food here will probably attract swarms of insects. The nearest village for refreshments is Salin-de-Giraud, but first try the B&Bs at Le Paradis or nearby St Bertrand.
How to get there: 🚗 to the pumping station between the Etang du Fangassier and the Etang de Galabert (accessible from Villeneuve on the D37 — the 146km-point in Car tour 6; see notes on pages 33-34). Outside winter, the car will be a furnace on your return.

This circuit on the north side of the Etang de Galabert is a good introduction to the Camargue, one of the very few places in the Mediterranean where flamingoes breed. Not only will you see your fill of flamingoes (45,000 individuals have been recorded here), but a great many other birds as well.

Start out at the PUMPING STATION between the **Galabert and Fangassier lagoons**. (The flamingoes breed on an islet in the Fangassier Lagoon, and from April to July their raised conical nests are under round-the-clock surveillance by the park and reserve authorities.) Follow the dyke (**Digue à la Mer**) northwest; the pump will be just on your left as you set off — churning away, with any luck. The lighthouse (Phare de la Gacholle) glimmers in the distance. Spiny glassworts (*Salicornia* species) predominate, peppered by the odd wizened-up daisies, thistles and purple-flowering knautia. The track is embedded with tiny, perfectly-formed sea shells. A fairly stagnant strip of water is on your left and a narrow sand-bar beyond it; this will be the return route. The muted pinks and purples in the still water and the dull greens and yellows of the surface algae create beautiful abstract patterns. By the side of the path an intermittent double row of wooden posts helps to shore up the dyke; a sludge of salty foam clings to them. The monotony is broken only by the screeching of myriad seagulls swirling above an islet to the left. Eventually you reach the **Pont de**

View back to the Phare de la Gacholle from the sand-bar

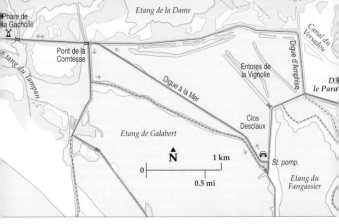

The salt-encrusted surface algae and the wooden retaining posts (ganivelles) create beautiful abstract patterns beside the path.

la **Comtesse** (**45min**), an important level-changing station. Cars are not allowed beyond this point, and walkers/cyclists are reminded to keep to the track. Passing the **Etang du Tampan** on the left, you come to the **Phare de la Gacholle** (**1h**), graced by a purple-flowering tamarisk, a fine specimen of the most characteristic tree in the Camargue. The surrounds of this lived-in lighthouse are closed. Return to the Pont de la Comtesse and turn right on a wide track.

Some 500m/yds along, be sure to turn left onto the sand-bar, not far beyond a barrier. (If you continue ahead, you would have to round the entire Etang de Galabert, a *very* long walk indeed.) This path, lined with gold grasses and sprouting huge yellow oyster plants with thistle-like leaves, runs down the middle of the sand-bar. While you wait for a flamingo to spread its black and salmon-red wings within camera range, be sure to watch your feet or you're likely to trip up on one of the hundreds of huge rabbit holes. Opposite 'shriek island', still swirling with gulls, you come across the colony of sneezeworts (*Achillea*) shown on page 87. When you approach the PUMPING STATION, turn right to cross a BRIDGE; then, about 20m/yds beyond it, turn left on a track, back to your car (**2h15min**).

Walk 16: MONTCALMES, AND A VIEW OVER ST-GUILHEM-LE-DESERT

Distance: 13.5km/8.4mi; 3h45min

Grade: easy-moderate, with ascents/descents of 175m/575ft overall. Stony tracks throughout, and virtually *no shade* en route. Variable waymarking: yellow PR flashes, red dots, green posts. *IGN maps 2643 E, 2743 O*

Equipment: see page 55; refreshments available at Puéchabon

How to get there: 🚗 to the Bergerie Neuve. Leave the D32 at the calvary on the south side of

Puéchabon (Car tour 7): head west on the road here, then turn right immediately on a narrow tarred road. Follow it for 2.3km, until it ends at a building (the Bergerie Neuve). Or 🚌 to Puéchabon and walk from there (add 6km/up to 1h30min return).

Short walk: Bergerie Neuve — Montcalmès — Bergerie Neuve. 5km/3mi; 1h05min. Easy climb and descent of 85m/280ft. Follow the main walk for 35min and return the same way.

This walk across a limestone plateau *(causse)* above the Gorges de l'Hérault takes us through *garrigues* bristling with holm and kermes oaks to the magnificent viewpoint over St-Guilhem-le-Désert shown on page 91. With each footstep we move back in time ... to the 8th century, when Charlemagne was on the throne.

Start out at the **Bergerie Neuve:** take the motorable track furthest to the left and climb to the hamlet of **Lavène** (**15min**). Today there are only a couple of inhabited buildings spilling out windowboxes fresh with colour, but in the 8th century Lavène was a *cité*. Continue on the main track, heading straight towards St-Baudille (with the large relay station, one of the peaks of the Séranne massif). Ten minutes along you pass a *lavogne* on the left-hand side of the

track (a paved watering hole for animals; **Lac Neuf** on the map). Just beyond it, at a Y-fork, keep right. This very stony track takes you to the ruined fortified hamlet of **Montcalmès** (**35min**). The huge château here also dates from the 8th century and was given by Charlemagne to St-Benoît. The very substantial remains include arches, doorways, a well-preserved *bergerie* and a baking oven. There is shade and grass; it makes a superb picnic spot, where you can

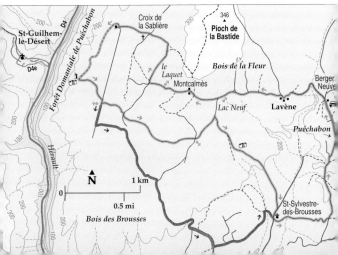

Lac Neuf (top left), baking oven at Moncalmès (above) and St-Sylvestre-des-Brousses (left)

end the Short walk. Be sure to explore the ruins *carefully;* some of the masonry is unstable. Continuing on the track, five minutes beyond Montcalmès you pass a second, semi-circular *lavogne* on the right (**Le Laquet**). Now St-Baudille and the mountains behind St-Guilhem seem very close indeed. Three minutes past the *lavogne* ignore a track off to the left. Half a minute later, ignore a second track off left; keep to the obvious main track, ignoring offshoots. You eventually pass an IRON CROSS on the left, some 30m/ yds away (**Croix de la Sablière; 55min**). The track runs alongside masses of small rock quarries before reaching the WESTERN EDGE OF THE PLATEAU (just over **1h05min**), from where the view towards the Séranne improves. There is a three-way fork here. Ignore the track straight ahead *and* the main track (marked with a huge cairn) which swings left and heads southwest in a straight line. Locate instead the small marker-stone to the right and take the narrow footpath to the right of it. This path quickly swings left and skirts the edge of the plateau. From time to time a cart track impinges on the path, but you can

see the TV relay where you are heading. Keep an eye out for the turpentine and mastic trees (*Pistacia terebinthus* and *Pistacia lentiscus*), growing amidst the holm and holly oaks. Their red-to-black berries feed the birds that winter here. Foliage has grown up around the RELAY STATION (**1h 30min**), so potter about until you can find an open viewpoint from which to savour the exquisite view shown opposite. St-Guilhem lies far below, a river of salmon-coloured rooftops flowing through the Combe de Gellone, below the menacing cliffs of the Cirque de l'Infernet. The rounded apse of the abbey church (all that remains of the original monastery founded by St-Guilhem) is clearly visible. (The church still displays its most precious relic — a piece of the true cross, given by Charlemagne to his friend Guilhem when the monastery was founded in 804.) Take the track leading away from the relay. In three minutes ignore a track off to the left; it rejoins your track a minute later (just past a small but deep PIT on the left). After another two minutes, join the main track and go right, coming to a GREEN WATER TANK with the sign '**Forêt Domaniale de Puéchabon**' on your right in one minute. Turn left here. (*The track straight ahead is an alternative, equally attractive route, indicated by a purple line on the map.*) Five minutes later, at a T-junction, turn right. A minute later ignore a track off right. You come to a crossing track, where there is another GREEN WATER TANK on the right (under **2h05min**); keep straight ahead here. Ignore a track on the right a minute later (it rejoins the main track). But six minutes past the water tank (**2h10min**), when you are almost back to the first *lavogne* on your outgoing route, turn right on a very stony track marked with a CAIRN (and a YELLOW FLASH about 20m/yds along).

This track rises slightly before descending steeply. There are fine views south to Aniane and the Hérault once you have cleared the trees and are approaching a vast spread of vineyards. Like the abbey church at St-Guilhem,

St-Sylvestre-des-Brousses (**2h50min**) was an important stop along the pilgrims' route to Santiago de Compostela. Head left downhill on the track behind the chapel. *(Or, if you came by the alternative route, keep straight ahead downhill.)* You climb to a crossing track, from where Puéchabon is visible to the right (**3h10min**). Turn left and keep climbing gently, now following RED WAY-MARKS (and GREEN POSTS). When you come to a fork, where the waymarking posts and a cairn direct you to the right, keep *left*. At the next fork, a minute later, go right. Rejoining the little lane to the *bergerie,* turn left back to the **Bergerie Neuve (3h45min).**

St-Guilhem, seen from the plateau

Walk 17: ON THE SHOULDERS OF PIC ST-LOUP

Distance: 4.5km/2.8mi; 2h
Grade: easy, gradual ascent/
descent of 200m/650ft on a very
stony track. Exploring the ruined
castle demands agility and a head
for heights (small children must
be supervised carefully). Little
shade. Some GR waymarking;
other sections *not* waymarked.
IGN map 2742 ET
Equipment: see page 55; refreshments available at St-Mathieu
How to get there: 🚗 to
St-Mathieu-de-Tréviers (a detour
from Car tour 7). Where Car tour
7 turns back at the fork to Valflaunès, keep ahead towards St-
Mathieu and, at the roundabout,
turn right on the D17. After
about 2km, at another roundabout, turn right on the D26e.

Follow a deep hairpin bend to the
left and, at the entrance to the
village, turn left. Then go left
again (in front of a large iron
gate). Now you are on a narrow
road which climbs to the Château
St-Aunès. At the entrance (🚩: *PIC
ST-LOUP, CHATEAU DE MONT-
FERRAND, ACCES PEDESTRE*), turn
right on the track (large parking
area 100m downhill).
**Alternative walk: Pic St-Loup
summit.** 6.5km/4mi; 3h30min.
Strenuous ascent/descent of
500m/1650ft; you must be sure-
footed. Follow the main walk to
the 35min-point, then keep left
on the GR. The final ascent
begins from the cross at **La Croi-
sette** and follows an old pilgrims'
trail to the chapel at the top.

There are several walks around Pic St-Loup, of which the
PR route shown on IGN maps rounding the mountain
and taking in the summit is probably the finest. But it takes a
good five-six hours, and there is very little shade in this area.
We prefer to look at the peak from a distance, from where its
fine spinnaker-shaped wedge of rock can best be appreciated.
This walk, to the Château de Montferrand, shows you the best
of Pic St-Loup and its twin, Hortus, as well as far-reaching
views to the Pyrenees and Mont Ventoux!

Start out at the PARKING AREA,
following the red and white flashes
of the GR60 (🚩) along a stony
track. You're into the climb
straight away. Just before a
concrete RESERVOIR (**5min**), turn
right up a stony trail through the
garrigues, where white Montepllier
cistus is particularly prominent.
Keep to the very stony GR,
ignoring any smaller paths off
right or left. From time to time
you will see the imposing château
ahead or catch glimpses of the
cross atop Pic St-Loup.
When you come to a small
CLEARING (**35min**), the GR continues ahead as an earthen path
(*Alternative walk*). Turn right
uphill here (*no* waymarking) on

another very stony trail. In three
minutes you come to a fork, where
you must turn *sharp left uphill* —
even though you can see the
château straight ahead. Two
minutes later make another hairpin
turn to the right, where a very
narrow path goes straight ahead.
You come to a fork with a LARGE
ROCK in the centre (**50min**), on
which a plea to not discard litter is
painted in blue. You *can* fork left
here and climb over the rubble for
a preliminary view over the plain
and to Hortus, but the best way
up to the ruins lies to the *right* of
the stone. This route leads to a
section of ruined wall where you
can get a foothold. From there a
fairly strong path leads *almost* all

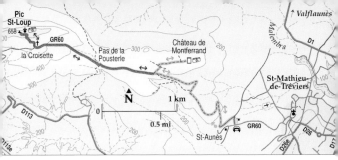

the way to the top. Clamber around the ruins of the **Château de Montferrand** (**1h**) carefully, admiring the vaulted rooftops remaining, the water deposits, the various keep walls.

From here you look north down into the lovely Terrieu Valley, where the cliffs of the Montagne d'Hortus rise behind Mas Rigaud. In the far distance the Cévennes shimmer in a blue haze. On a clear day, Mont Ventoux is visible in the east while, to the west, beyond the shoulder of St-Loup, you can see the huge relay station on St-Baudille in the Séranne massif (photograph page 91), and the Pyrenees in the far distance. In the south you overlook the plains of Montpellier all the way to the coast and the buildings of La Grande Motte. Swallows swoop all round you.

This château was one of seven which Raymond VI of Toulouse was forced to surrender during the crusade against the Albigensians (see box page 49).

When you decide to leave, be sure you redescend via the wall with the foothold. (If you find yourself on what appears to be a good but stony path descending due south, you have gone wrong. This path *does* rejoin the GR, but it is very difficult.) Retrace your steps to the PARKING AREA (**2h**).

Pic St-Loup from the Château de Montferrand (left); the Terrieu Valley, with St-Loup at the left and Hortus to the right

Walk 18: SOURCE OF THE VIS

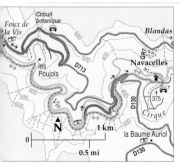

Grade: fairly easy, with ascents/descents of about 100m/330ft overall. A few stretches demand agility. Some red and white GR waymarking, some local blue waymarking. *IGN map 2642 ET*

Equipment: see page 55; swimming things; refreshments available in Navacelles

How to get there: 🚍 to the *auberge* in Navacelles (Car tour 8)

Short walk: Banks of the Vis. 4km/2.5mi; 1h10min. Grade as main walk. Follow the main walk for about 35min and return the same way.

See also photographs pages 8-9 and 40-41
Distance: 8km/5mi; 2h40min

This walk is perfect for a hot day; there's some shade en route, and the surging source of the river Vis at the end of the walk is blissfully cooling. This crystal-clear river is also an ideal swimming-hole, so take a picnic and plan to spend much of the day by its banks.

Start out at the *auberge* in **Navacelles**. Cross the road to the POST BOX, where there is a GR waymark on the wall ahead. Take the lane at the left of the post box (GR ▪: BLANDAS 4,5KM). The lane skirts to the left of the river. Take the first left turn off the lane (sign: GITE D'ETAPE). Pass the CHURCH on the right and continue uphill on a narrow lane, walking to the right of a rounded wall with a waymark. When you come to the road, turn right. This slog up tarmac is unpleasant in hot weather, but you quickly come to the top of the climb, at a junction (**10min**). Here the D130 goes left to St-Maurice and the D713 ahead to Blandas. In between them is a footpath (▪: FOUX DE LA VIS 1H), indicating that the source of the Vis is 1h away (for the *very* fleet of foot!).
Follow the path; it's marked with blue paint and leads you gently downhill past bright yellow broom, which flowers from April to July. After passing above a DAM (**20min**) the undulating path

narrows. Sometimes you are quite high above the river so, although the drop is not sheer, watch your footing. Various bell-flowers are among the flora brightening this shady bower. Ten minutes later you descend very steeply to a T-junction with another path, where you turn left.
This is a lovely earthen path, pleasantly free of stones for the moment. The river is singing over on your right and, a minute along, you join it at a GRASSY VERGE (**35min**), a fine picnic spot. But before you settle for the day, continue just a short way further — to another gorgeous spot, where flat slabs of rock jut out into the river (unless the river is running very high). This is an ideal spot to launch yourself for a swim and sunbathe afterwards. Damsel- and dragonflies in fluorescent hues dart about here, vying with the cornflower blue, orange, and yellow butterflies for attention; but most spectacular are the moths, their wings an intricate pattern of scarlet, teal blue and

94

black. Until you reach the source, this is the most beautiful part of the walk.

Soon the path is somewhat overgrown and climbs away from the river. Eventually you pass the abandoned farmhouse of **Les Poujols** on the right (**1h05min**). On cool days, this open area makes a pleasant sun-trap for a picnic. A magnificent cedar forest comes into view on the opposite riverbank ten minutes later. (A *Circuit botanique* signposted from the D713 descends to the source through this forest; see Car tour 8 and purple lines on the map.) Ten minutes past Les Poujols, turn right downhill (▪: *LA FOUX;* **1h15min**). It's a steep descent of a few minutes to an old mill, from where you'll have to scramble for another minute to enjoy the view of the source shown below. The atmosphere in this roaring green cauldron is wonderfully invigorating.

As you climb back up from the source, the enormous cliffs of the Causse du Larzac tower above you. In 45 minutes you will be back at the place where rocks jut out into the river. Just past the grassy verge, *be sure to climb uphill to the right on your outgoing path;* there *are* waymarks here, but they are easily missed. (The path straight ahead, indicated on the map by a purple line, leads to a ford over to the dam passed earlier and then a track out onto the road, but the river can only be forded in summer.)

In 1h10min from the mill you should be back at the road junction. If you are staying overnight in Navacelles (apart from the *auberge,* there is also a *gîte d'étape*), and you do this walk late in day, you'll come back into the village hugging yourself with the knowledge that you have this whole magnificent amphitheatre *almost* all to yourself. High up to the right, on the plateau, you can spot the farm of La Baume Auriol, from where you probably first saw the *cirque.* When the road curves round, and the statue on the hillock in the 'moat' is just ahead of you, turn down the tarred lane that you climbed at the start of the walk. Retrace your steps to the *auberge* in **Navacelles** (**2h40min**).

The Vis surges through a ruined 18th-century mill at its source. Incredibly, this torrent suddenly ceased in April 1776. One can imagine the fear of the local people — who not only depended upon the Vis, but upon the mighty Hérault, which it feeds. Eight days later, as inexplicably as it had ceased, the source boiled over its cauldron again.

Walk 19: MONTPELLIER-LE-VIEUX

See also photograph page 2
Distance: 5.5km/3.4mi; 2h15min
Grade: moderate ups and downs of about 150m/490ft, requiring agility. Good shade. Multi-coloured waymarking. *IGN map 2641 OT*
Equipment: see page 55; nearest refreshments point: Millau
How to get there: 🚌 to Montpellier-le-Vieux (a detour on Car tour 7; see page 41). Paid parking includes a plan, but *note:* their plan has *south* at the top.

Photograph: Cirque de la Millière

Montpellier-le-Vieux is a *ruiniform* chaos writ large — so impressive that E-A Martel mapped the site. Our suggested walk takes in four of the five different routes (waymarked with coloured cubes on the ground). Pack a picnic and plan to spend at least half a day enjoying not only the rock formations, but the splendid woodlands and luxuriant displays of mosses, ferns ... and wild flowers in spring.

Start out at the PARKING AREA: go up the path (■: CIRCUITS). At a fork, take the RED PATH left to the **Douminal** (**15min**), a rock tower overlooking the four *cirques* of the chaos. In the north is the thickly-forested Cirque du Lac, with the Tarn cliffs rising in the distance. From here *retrace your steps* to the RED/BLUE PATH and follow it to the left **Belvédère** (**40min**), overlooking the **Cirque de la Millière**. Walk back over the bridge and turn right on the RED PATH, following it *across* the turning circle for the little train and a pleasant picnic area on the right. Ignore the purple path off to the right here but, a minute later, fork right on the YELLOW PATH. The **Roc Camparolié** is the most dramatic formation on this stretch. Pass a narrow path off to the right (not signposted; it leads to the village of La-Roque-Ste-Marguerite in 1h), then descend to a clearing, where the **Arc de Triomphe** is ahead. Just past here, at a T-junction, go right (passing the **Crocodile** up on the right. From the **Sphinx** (**1h25min**), curl hard left to the **Porte de Mycènes** (a good picnic area).
Return to the Sphinx but, just before it, take the narrow ORANGE PATH, past the **Eléphant**. When you come to a Y-fork, keep left through the picnic area overlooking the **Cirque du Lac**, then fork right on the BLUE/RED PATH, back to the CAR PARK (**2h15min**).

Montpellier-le-Vieux

(map)

Cirque du Lac
Salle des Fêtes
Cénotaphe
Tête d'Arlequin
l'Amphore
le Chameau
Rocher de la Croix
l'Oule
Tombeaux
Victoria
Douminal
836
la Poterne
Tête d'Ours
Grotte de la
Baume obscure
Rempart
l'Eléphant
Aven
la Quille
Belvédère
Cirque des Rouquettes
Nez de Cyrano
Porte de Mycènes
le Sphinx
Chaise curule
le Crocodile
Rochers de Château Gaillard
Arc de Triomphe
Cirque de la Millière
N
300 m
Cirque des Amats
Roc Camparolié

Walk 20: SENTIER DE LA VALLEE DU TARN

Distance: 7km/4.3mi; 2h35min
Grade: easy, with a short ascent/descent of 60m/200ft. You must be sure-footed. Green and yellow waymarking. *IGN map 2640 OT*
Equipment: see page 55; swimming things. Refreshments available at La Malène
How to get there: 🚌 to La Malène, halfway along the Gorges du Tarn (a detour on Car tour 7;

see page 41), or 🚐
Alternative walk: La Malène — St-Chély. 10km/6.2mi; 3h30min. Grade as main walk. Follow the main walk to Hautrives, then continue along the riverside path to St-Chély, from where you can return to La Malène by taxi or bus.
Stroll/picnic suggestion: Banks of the Tarn. Follow the walk to the 15min-point and back.

La Malène, at the junction of roads connecting the Sauveterre and Méjean *causses,* was a focal point for the *transhumance* for centuries. Today it makes an ideal centre for exploring the Gorges du Tarn. Not only do the boat trips to the Cirque des Baumes leave from here, but it's an ideal spot to take in two splendid walks. This first ramble makes an superb early-morning or late-afternoon stroll to one of the prettiest hamlets in the area — Hauterives.

Start out at the CAR PARK in **La Malène.** Cross the BRIDGE (passing the TOURIST OFFICE on your left), and turn left on the road to the Col de Rieisse. After 30m/yds, turn left down a path marked with green and yellow flashes — the **Sentier de la Vallée du Tarn.** This is an exceptionally pretty stretch of the long-distance path, but it's *very* narrow in places (only

about 30cm/12in), so *do* watch your footing. After passing some RAPIDS and just 30m/yds beyond a CONCRETE BRIDGE with an iron railing on one side, you come to a small *GRASSY SHELF* at the water's edge (**15min**) — an idyllic spot, where you can picnic with your feet in the water.
About 800m/0.5mi short of Hauterives, the path gains 60m of

On the approach to Hauterives; see also photograph page 100.

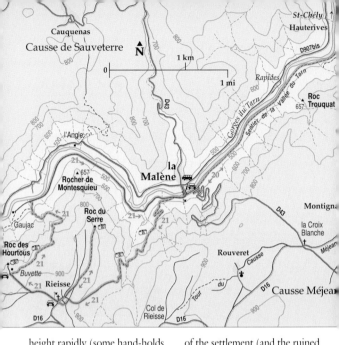

height rapidly (some hand-holds are necessary). Then it descends again to **Hauterives** (**1h20min**), one of several beautifully-restored Caussenard hamlets along the banks of the Tarn. The upper part of the settlement (and the ruined castle) can be reached by a path just past the houses. But the main walk turns back from the riverside hamlet; retrace your steps to **La Malène** (**2h35min**).

Walk 21: ROC DES HOURTOUS

See map opposite
Distance: 9km/5.6mi; 3h50min
Grade: fairly strenuous, with ascents/descents of 500m/1640ft overall. Most of the paths are excellent, but the steep descent requires surefootedness and can be very slippery when wet. Yellow waymarking. *IGN map 2640 OT*
Equipment: see page 55; refreshments available at La Malène, Rieisse and the seasonal *buvette* at the Roc des Hourtous
How to get there: 🚌 to La Malène (see page 97), or 🚐
Short walks: both are easy; access by car: take the *difficult* hairpin road (D43) from La Malène towards the COL DE RIEISSE. Turn

right at a crossroads (La Croix Blanche) on the D16 and, beyond the Col de Rieisse, turn right again towards Rieisse village.

1 Roc du Serre. 35min return. Park at the junction with a cross, at the edge of Rieisse (sign: PANORAMA ROC DU SERRE). Follow the main walk from the 1h40minpoint to the viewpoint and return the same way.

2 Roc des Hourtous. 30min return. Continue past Rieisse following PANORAMA DES HOURTOUS. Park near the *buvette* (open from May to October). Follow the main walk from the 2h35min- to the 2h50min-point and return the same way.

O ne of the most spectacular walks in the Tarn, this is an ideal day's outing. Fortunately there is plenty of shade, so the walk is possible even at the height of summer. The views from the top are among the finest in the Tarn. The less energetic can see the best of the sights in the Short walks but, while it's easier on the legs and lungs, the drive up to Rieisse (on ten hairpin bends) is not for the faint-hearted!

The stupendous outlook to the north from the Roc des Hourtous, with the Tarn below and the Causse de Sauveterre opposite. This viewpoint is just above Les Détroits (not shown in the photograph), the narrowest part of the gorge, where the sheer cliffs rise 400m/1300ft from the river. It's hard to believe, but in the early 1990s a French tightrope walker had a 1km-long cable strung across the gorge from these cliffs. He crossed it on foot and returned on a motorbike, with his wife suspended in a basket!

Sentier de la Vallée du Tarn(Walks 20 and 21)

Start out at the CAR PARK in **La Malène**. Cross the BRIDGE (passing the TOURIST OFFICE on your left), and turn right on a track (➽: *ROC DES HOURTOUS*). After 150m/yds, turn left up a path marked with yellow flashes. Although there is plenty of shady foliage, you will come to several viewpoints back over La Malène's setting as you climb. The path rises in easy zigzags — relatively speaking — minimising the tiring ascent of 450m/1475ft.

After a final pull to the top of the **Causse Méjean** you come into the village of **Rieisse**. Follow the waymarks up to a junction with a STONE CROSS dated 1739 (**1h 40min**) and turn right (➽: *PANO-RAMA ROC DU SERRE*). Walk along the lane (closed to cars) and keep right at three Y-forks, always following the main grassy, later earthen track.

From the **Roc du Serre** (**2h**)you enjoy a plunging view back down over La Malène and the comings and goings along the river, over to the Causse de Sauveterre, and back to the *lacets* of the D43 snaking up to the Causse Méjean.

Return to the stone cross and now take the motorable track to the right (sign: *PANORAMA DES HOURTOUS*). The waymarked path turns off the track to pass to the right of the *buvette* at the **Roc des Hourtous** (**2h35min**), then edges the plateau. This entire stretch, with springy moss underfoot, is incredibly beautiful in spring — an 'Easter basket' of blue, purple and yellow flowers, including several species of orchids. Although the mixed woodlands are thick, there are several promontories with splendid outlooks. You are just east of Les Détroits, the narrowest part of the gorge. Looking back, your view encompasses the Cirque des Baumes and the Point Sublime in the west.

After 800m/0.5mi, watch for your left turn down a narrow footpath (**2h50min**) which demands careful footwork.

Once back down at the RIVERSIDE (**3h20min**), turn right and follow the track (**Sentier de la Vallée du Tarn**) back to **La Malène** (**3h50min**).

Walk 22: CHATEAU DE MALAVIEILLE AND LA LIEUDE

Distance: 10km/6.2mi; 3h10min
Grade: easy-moderate, with ascents/descents of 300m/1000ft overall. Some agility is required at the château. Good surfaces underfoot, but no shade. Yellow waymarking. *IGN map 2643 O*
Equipment: see page 55; refreshments available at nearby Octon
How to get there: 🚗 to Malavieille (Car tour 9, page 42). Park 0.5km beyond the sign denoting the end of Malavieille (⌐ on the right: ST-FULCRAN, PRADELS, LE CASTELAS, LA LIEUDE). Or 🚌 to Octon and walk from there (add 8km/5mi; 2h return).
Short walk: Le Castelas. 1.6km/1mi; 50min. Grade as main walk (ascent/descent 150m/500ft). Park 2km beyond Malavieille, at the path up to the ruined château *(castelas)*.

This beautiful walk is also interesting from a geological point of view. We cross a landscape of *ruffes* (see caption overleaf) and climb a 'thimble' of basalt, recalling the volcanic origins of the area. Embedded in this burgundy-red soil are fossilized animal prints dating from the Permian Period.

Start out at the PARKING AREA: walk north along the asphalted track. On coming to a fork, go half left; don't continue straight ahead. You descend into a little valley and pass the ruins of the 15th-century **Chapelle St-Fulcran (15min)**, dedicated to Lodève's patron saint. Keep straight ahead past the chapel, at first following electricity wires.
In **20min** the way curves left up an old stone-laid trail, to mount the flanks of the **Montagne de la Boutine**. As you climb in deep zigzags there are fine views of the plain below, especially the vineyards in the southwest (where the photograph on page 43 was taken). **Pradels (40min)** is a honey-coloured huddle of stone houses. Leave the hamlet on a

narrow concrete lane, continuing along the mountainside. Soon you enjoy the view shown overleaf: you look straight down the deep **Rieupeyre Valley** to the silhouette of the *castelas* (Château de Malavieille) on the far side. In spring the lime-green hillsides are ablaze with bright yellow broom.
The highest point of the walk is soon reached (spot height 431m; **1h**). From here you look out right to Le Mas Bas and Brenas, rising from a patchwork quilt of fields. Turn left and descend due south towards the *castelas* on another lane (the road continues to Le Mas Bas). The concrete gives way to a delightful grassy trail. Look to your left now: on the far side of the Rieupeyre Valley, wine-red *ruffes* stream vertically down the

101

Looking south along the Rieupeyre Valley to the silhouette of the Château de Malavieille in the distance. This area, near Lake Salagou, is famous for its ruffes — furrows of clay-bearing limestone soil. The striking contrast between the spring-green grass and this red soil is one of the highlights of the walk.
Left: the castelas, *the ruined Château de Malavieille*

hillsides through the broom, almost like lava flows.

When you pass a BARN on the right (**1h20min**) and come upon a cultivated field, walk along the left-hand edge of the field and then curve round to the right. Now locate the *very clear* earthen path to the ruins, on your left (be sure to find it, or you will end up lacerated by brambles). Scramble up into the ruined 12th-/13th-century *castelas* (**Château de Malavieille; 1h35min**) and enjoy the panorama and your picnic lunch. On the very steep, stony descent watch for the waymarks indicating the best footholds. You descend to a SHELTER housing fossilised imprints of *Thereapsides*, precursors of mammals. They lived in this area, where there is thought to have been a watering-hole, some 250 million years ago (a long time before the dinosaurs). They were probably furry and warm-blooded. The prints are hard to see at first, until you realise that these were *not* large animals. The largest of them was only about 3m/12ft long, the smallest 50cm/under 2ft.
102

With your back to the shelter, head right along the road to **La Lieude** (**2h05min**). Just past the last house *on the left*, turn left down an earthen path (waymark after a dozen paces). Cross a stream and go ahead on a two-wheeled track, crossing another bridge a minute later. A short climb follows: bear left at a fork (waymark on a rock). From here there is a good view towards Lake Salagou and back to the ruins and the Rieupeyre Valley. Come to a T-junction and turn left (the **Villetelle** farm is on the right). At the next fork go right uphill, heading between fields towards some cypresses.

On reaching **Le Mas Canet** (**2h45min**) turn left. At an intersection, where there is a CROSS on the right, continue straight ahead. Meet the D8: turn left towards BRENAS and OCTON but, after 200m/yds, go right on a narrow tarmac lane (the first one you come to). Not long after crossing a CONCRETE FORD you reach **Malavieille** and turn left back to the PARKING AREA (**3h10min**).

Walk 23: CIRQUE DE MOUREZE AND MONTAGNE DE LIAUSSON

Distance: 5.5km/3.4mi; 2h35min	**Equipment:** see page 55; refreshments available in Mourèze
Grade: easy-moderate, with an initial climb of 300m/1000ft. The paths in the *cirque* are very stony underfoot — ankle-twisting terrain. Some agility is needed. Little shade en route. Varied waymarking colours. *IGN map 2643 O*	**How to get there:** 🚗 to Mourèze (Car tour 9). Or 🚐 to Mourèze.
	Short walk: Cirque de Mourèze. Allow 1h. Grade as main walk, but ups and downs of about 100m/330ft. Just visit the *cirque*.

Not only does this walk explore the extraordinary Cirque de Mourèze from all angles, but from the Montagne de Liausson you enjoy the best possible view over the Lac du Salagou, one of the most famous beauty spots in Hérault.

Begin the walk on the main road in **Mourèze**, just east of the CHURCH; follow ☞ DIRECTION DU CIRQUE along a tarred lane. Turn left towards the church at the first alley, and then turn right. After passing the last house, you come to a fork; ignore the left-hand path signposted to the Col des Portes (it is your return route). Keep straight ahead (the right-hand fork). There are no waymarks here, but head towards the right of the large PILLARS OF ROCK straight in front of you, and you will soon pick up BLUE FLASH WAYMARKS. The main path runs in a ROCKY CLEFT (**10min**) just below and to the right of these pillars. Follow the waymarks carefully. When you are about 100m/yds or so short of the Sphinx (the rock formation shown at the right), waymarks direct you to the left — into another narrow cleft in the rock. This stretch takes you below and just to the left of the **Sphinx** (**15min**).

Eventually the path veers to the right, edging towards Mount Liausson. When you come to a T-junction (spot height 317m; **35min**), ignore the old charcoal burners' path to the right; turn *left*. Some 20 paces up this path, a tree on left is waymarked with *red and blue* flashes; follow this new waymarking up the mountain. The

path is fairly steep, but not very stony, and it is pleasantly shaded by holm oaks. You gain height quickly and easily, at the same time enjoying ever-improving views to the south over Mourèze and its *cirque,* the Pic de Vissou (with the transmitter), and the distant sea. Caroux and the Espinouse rise in the west.

At the SUMMIT of the **Montagne de Liausson** (523m/1720ft; **1h**)

The Sphinx

103

Mourèze church

you reach the viewpoint shown below, with the Causse du Larzac and the Cévennes in the distance. From here head west along the crest, following *yellow* waymarks. You pass to the right of the ruined priory of **St-Jean d'Aureillan** and then reach a SECOND SUMMIT (535m; **1h20min**). This is a fine viewpoint over the dolomitic pillars in the *cirque* and the maze of blinding-white paths that wind through it. The (sometimes awkward) descent to the Col des Portes begins here. At a fork 15 minutes downhill be sure to go right (BLUE ARROW); the path down to the left leads to some more interesting dolomitic formations, but is a cul-de-sac. (Allow *double* the time on the signposts, if you take any diversions!)
At the **Col des Portes** (**1h50min**)

arrows point in all directions. Turn down left (⊩: MOUREZE). Ten minutes downhill, at a major junction where two trees are surrounded by rocks and a track goes off to the right, turn left downhill on a track (towards the Pic de Vissou). Then leave this track after just four minutes: go left on a footpath waymarked in blue (spot height 280m). It brings you back into the *cirque* just north of the ruined CASTLE. Huge rock pillars soon tower above you, as you battle your way through a tall forest of pungent broom. At **2h25min** you're back at the fork you first encountered at the start of the walk. Turn right, to pass the CHURCH and return to the main road in **Mourèze** (**2h35min**).

Liausson and the Lac du Salagou from the summit of Mount Liausson

Walk 24: GORGES D'HERIC

Distance: 11km/6.8mi; 4h
Grade: moderate-strenuous, with ascents/descents of 500m/1640ft overall (400m/1310ft at the outset). Excellent surfaces underfoot. Blue, red, and red and white GR waymarking. *IGN map 2543 O*
Equipment: see page 55; refreshments available at Mons and halfway through the walk, at Héric
How to get there: 🚌 to Mons, above La Trivalle (Car tour 9); park near the church. Or 🚐 to La Trivalle, from where you must climb to Mons (0.8km/0.5mi; 15min each way).

Short walks: Both start at the TOURIST OFFICE at **Mons-la-Trivalle** on the D908, where you board the 'Petit Train' for an excursion up the Gorges d'Héric (operates all year round). Alight at the Gouffre du Cerisier, halfway up the gorge, and arrange with the driver to be collected again when he makes a later run.

1 Gouffre du Cerisier — Héric — Gouffre du Cerisier. 7km/4.3mi; 2h. Easy ascent/descent of 150m/500ft. Follow the concrete lane to the isolated mountain hamlet of Héric (refreshments), then descend to the Gouffre du

Cerisier for your return train.

2 Gouffre du Cerisier — Parking. 3km/2mi; 1h. Very easy descent on a concrete lane. From the Gouffre walk back down the gorge to the parking area, and pick up the train there for the return to Mons-la-Trivalle.

Whether you only do the short stroll down from the Gouffre du Cerisier or you huff and puff up to Héric and back, you can anticipate a glorious and rewarding day out. Your physical needs are catered for with plenty of shade and beautifully-surfaced paths underfoot. Spiritually the walk is as fulfilling as a symphony, with lofty peaks piercing the clouds above you, an emerald-green river bouncing down beside you, and the trill of bird-song.

Start out at the CHURCH in **Mons**. Climb the narrow road just opposite it, heading up a narrow alley towards an arch (BLUE FLASHES on an electricity pole on the left). Go under the arch and turn left in front of the *gîte*, into another alley. Curve round to the right uphill on a concrete lane. When you reach a SHED/GARAGE straight in front of

you (**5min**), turn right, passing a house on the left. At the far edge of the house, turn left up steps, to begin climbing an old stone-laid trail waymarked with *BLUE TRI-ANGLES AND RED FLASHES*. If the owners of the house have scattered some belongings across the path, don't worry that you have stumbled into a private garden;

This bridge over the Vialais (a tributary of the Héric) is an ideal swimming and picnicking spot. If you are only doing Short walk 1, you can reach it in under 10 minutes from Héric, by following signposting to Bardou.

just forge ahead. One minute along, the trail forks: go left. When the trail crosses the bed of the **Ruisseau de Roujas** (**25-30min**), you may notice some blue paint waymarks enticing you up the bouldery stream bed. *Ignore them.* Keep left, following the BLUE TRIANGLES AND RED FLASHES. The reason for the superb stone-laid trail is soon apparent: myriad walls and a broad-leafed canopy overhead testify to intensive cultivation of the chestnut tree in the past. If you come in early summer, when the berries have fallen to the ground and lie squashed in pools of black juice, you'll also notice the mulberry trees, with their oval,

serrated leaves. Mulberry trees were introduced (especially around Ganges) as early as the 13th century, to develop the silkworm industry; the caterpillars fed on mulberry leaves.

A huge CAIRN on the right announces the **Col de la Maure** (**1h05min**). Continue uphill, in 10 minutes passing to the left of another large CAIRN. When you reach a fork at the **Col du Reynard** (**1h30min**) *keep right*, even though the blue triangle and red flash waymarks waymarks turn down to the left. Follow the path with the BLUE 'X' on a tree. (The waymarks lead down to Bardou, but we pass *above* the hamlet.)

When the GR7 path comes up from behind on the left (from Bardou; **1h40min**), keep ahead, almost immediately coming to the **Col de Bardou**. Here a stony path goes ahead uphill and the GR, our ongoing route, turns down to the right beneath more chestnuts. Before taking it, follow the path ahead for a few minutes, then climb over bedrock to the iron railings. From this superb viewpoint you look out to a prominent 'hoof'-shaped double peak higher up the valley, over towards Héric and down along the gorge. Returning to the Col de Bardou (**1h55min**), now follow the GR quite steeply downhill. You cross the **Vialais Stream** on the bridge shown opposite (**2h20min**). At a fork almost immediately after the bridge, turn left uphill, past another stream. Soon signposts announce the *buvette* at **Héric** (**2h35min**) and our ongoing route (towards DOUCH). Handily, the path leads straight through the outdoor terrace of the café. So stop awhile, under the flowering ash, the fig, or the false acacia. Then continue to the concrete track on the far side of the terrace and turn right downhill (the GR7 climbs a path to the left here, to continue to Douch). Some 25 minutes downhill, you look straight up ahead at a needle of rock called **La Belle**; the Col de la Maure, where you encountered the first big cairn, is just to left of it. Further down, the jagged, green-tinged peaks of the **Cirque de Farrières** ahead seem to cut off our ongoing route, but the track bends round and crosses a FIRST BRIDGE (**3h**). Beyond a SECOND BRIDGE we come to the **Gouffre du Cerisier** (**3h05min**), where a large pool on the right is fed by a lovely waterfall. The little tourist 'train' turns round here. A THIRD BRIDGE is crossed just below an impressive escarpment much

Top: Cirque des Farrières; above: Héric, below the Espinouse massif

favoured by rock-climbers. Beyond a FOURTH BRIDGE (**3h25min**) we leave the gorge. Ignore the road down left into the car park: keep straight ahead for two minutes, then turn sharp right uphill on a concrete path (passing a *gîte* called Le Caroux on your right). The path skirts to the right of a VINEYARD. Where a track comes up from the left, turn right uphill on a wider path, still beside vineyards on your left. In 15 minutes, where a path comes in from behind to the right, keep ahead (left). Under five minutes later, at another T-junction amidst the houses of **Mons**, turn left downhill to the road, then go right, back to the CHURCH (**4h**).

Walk 25: CIRCUIT ABOVE OLARGUES

See also photograph page 44
Distance: 9km/5.6mi; 2h10min
Grade: fairly easy, with an initial
ascent of 150m/500ft. Good
surfaces underfoot. No *reliable*
waymarking; *follow the notes below
carefully!* IGN maps 2543 O,
2544 O
Equipment: see page 55; refreshments available at Olargues
How to get there: 🚗 to
Olargues. Park in the parking area
by the river, at the western end of
the village (Car tour 9). Or 🚐 to
Olargues.

This walk in the foothills of the Monts de l'Espinouse is both easy and rewarding. There are several fine view-points en route, but other corners of interest as well, like the delightful chapel of 'St Martin of the Eggs' shown opposite. At the end of the walk you might like to climb the 11th-century bell tower, for its fine panorama, unimpeded by trees.

The walk begins at the CAR PARK in **Olargues**, where the ancient **Pont du Diable** (1202) spans the Jaur. Cross the MODERN BRIDGE leading to the D908 and turn right. Then turn left uphill on the narrow concrete road on the far side of the PETROL STATION, rising in a northwesterly direction up to the little **Cesse Valley**. Vineyards stretch away to your left, and purple bellflowers line the road-side. You may spot some faded blue waymarks.

The road dips and you come to a T-junction (**15min**), where there is a POST BOX ahead. Go uphill to the right here, in the direction of Caroux above the Gorges d'Héric (setting for Walk 24). The concrete gives way to track, and you pass beside more vineyards, keeping them to the left. Soon you're climbing through chestnuts as well as cherry trees and vines. At a Y-fork (**30min**), go right uphill. Five minutes later you are just opposite the village of Mas du Gua. The bare rock edges of the Espinouse massif rise above you

here, but it is always to the high rock escarpment beyond the Gorges d'Héric that the eye is drawn. When you come to a fork (**38min**), go left. Now you will enjoy a fine view to the right over vineyards and eastwards along the valleys of the Jaur and Orb. The triangular peak at the far end of the valley is Tantajo, near Béda-rieux (Car tour 9).

The tiny chapel of **St-Martin-des-Oeufs** (**42min**) on the right bears the date 1889. Just past this chapel, turn right to follow the (upper) grassy trail through a lovely chestnut wood, the **Bois de Salan**, passing above a stone hut immediately. Foxgloves brighten this shady bower in early summer. Three minutes past the chapel, at a Y-fork, bear right down into the **Combe des Codouls**. A small BRIDGE is crossed and, two minutes later, you meet the concrete road from Les Sagnes: turn right downhill. Ignore roads and tracks coming in from the right, and soon enjoy a fine view straight ahead, towards the bell

108

Above: view east to the priory of St-Julien on the descent back towards Olargues. On the right is the long valley of the Jaur and the Orb. Right: the walls of St-Martin-des-Oeufs are decorated with charming frescoes.

tower on its wooded knoll. Notice how the red roof tiles in **Le Cros** (**1h05min**) are weighted down with stones as a protection against the *mistral*. This largish hamlet also boasts a marvellous view over the Jaur Valley and Olargues. Two minutes later, at the sign denoting the entrance to the hamlet, don't go straight ahead past the village wash house; curl downhill in a U-turn to the left, into a pretty glen, and cross a BRIDGE over a healthy stream.

A couple of minutes later keep right at a fork. After another three minutes (some 300m/yds beyond the bridge; **1h15min**), you come to a road junction: turn right downhill, passing to the right of a modern stone building built in traditional style. Straight ahead now, on the far side of vineyards, is the **Prieuré de St-Julien**. When the road bends to the right, go left uphill on a concrete path, passing to the right of a BARN. At another fork, where a farm track goes left (**1h25min**), curve round on concrete, making a a U-turn to the right. At the next fork, four

minutes later, where a track goes left into vineyards, keep right, coming onto concrete again. From here there is a splendid view up to Caroux and along to where Tantajo punctuates the end of the valley. At the three-way junction that comes up three minutes later, ignore the tracks straight ahead and to the right: go left downhill, following the electricity wires on your right. Just after passing a plantation of firs, the priory seems within arm's reach.

Go right at the next fork, after five minutes passing a cypress-studded CEMETERY below on the left and walking straight towards the bell tower. Olive trees border this stretch of track. When you meet the the D14e (**1h50min**), turn left downhill. Cross the D908 and the bridge over the Jaur. Walk left uphill towards CENTRE VILLE, then take the first lane up right into **Olargues**. Stroll east, back to the CAR PARK (**2h10min**).

Walk 26: CIRCUIT ABOVE ST-PONS

Distance: 9km/5.6mi; 2h40min
Grade: easy-moderate, with ascents/descents of 300m/1000ft overall. Good paths and tracks underfoot, but the descent into St-Pons is quite steep and stony. The waymarks (wooden posts, blue dots) are most easily followed in the direction described. *IGN map 2444 E*
Equipment: see page 55; refreshments available at St-Pons
How to get there: 🚌 to St-Pons. Park in the Place Forail, near the cathedral (Car tours 9, 10). Or 🚐 or 🚐 to St-Pons
Short walk: D907 above Brassac — St-Pons. 4.5km/2.8mi; 1h 30min. Easy, but a short, steep descent into St-Pons. Access with friends or taxi to the starting point: drive north on the D907 towards LA SALVETAT. About 0.8km past the turn-off left for Brassac, watch for two stone pillars on the right (sign: CAMPING VERT). Start here by picking up the main walk at the 1h10min-point.

Here's a lovely and varied ramble, ideal for a morning or afternoon. You start out along a burbling stream and climb in shade to the foothills of the Somail massif. Picking up the old 'road' from La Salvetat to St-Pons, you stride out across a grassy ridge — drenched in yellow broom in spring or purple heather in summer and autumn.

Start out at the **Place Forail**, the junction of the D907 and N112. Walk north on the D907. Where the road curves right (by a sign advising whether the Col du Cabarétou is open), you will see a WALKERS' INFORMATION BOARD on the left. The route we follow is the short version of the **Chemin des Sangliers** (Wild Boars' Trail). It is waymarked with wooden posts — some bearing the figure of a wild boar, others an arrow (>). Cross the BRIDGE here and go right up a tarred road, with the hexagonal façade of a large building on your left and the PARK with its tall wooden 'totem pole'-style sculpture on your right. At a fork (**5min**), keep straight uphill for HOPITAL (boar ▐, also white paint waymarks). When the road goes left (**6min**), head right on the **Traverse de Semmen**. At a Y-fork (**7min**) go left. Ignore a tarred road up left to houses; keep ahead on a shady track (**9min**). You pass the farm of **St-Mens** on the far side of the stream and then a tarmac lane comes in from a bridge on your right; keep ahead now, on the tarmac (▐>). Beyond a house (**Les Foulons**) you cross a bouncing STREAM (▐8). When the lane turns right uphill to another house, keep ahead on a cart track (▐, also red and yellow paint waymarks).

The track ends at two buildings (**Cabrol**; **25min**). Curl round to the left of the post (▐>) and follow the shady earthen footpath uphill. A STREAM runs about 4m/ 12ft over to your right. The path eventually curves left, away from the stream, and emerges on a track (**40min**; boar ▐ opposite). Turn right here. After 250m/yds this track makes a hairpin bend to the right. Go straight ahead on a lesser track (boar ▐). Meeting a fork at once, keep right; then ignore a track to the right. You pass to the right of TWO HUTS.

Four minutes later you come to a road, near a SIGN DENOTING THE ENTRANCE TO **Brassac** (**50min**). Walk left along the road, to a post (▐>). Go downhill towards Brassac, pass a farm building on the right and then, two minutes from joining the road, turn right

110

On the descent back to St-Pons

on a track. (There are *two* tracks on your right here; the one to take is the first, lower track, which follows a stream. At this point you *leave* the 'boar' signposts, to follow the short version of the Sangliers circuit. The signpost bears a different symbol — perhaps meant to be a boar's hoofprint? At a fork, keep right on a higher, grassy track (▐). The track narrows to a beautiful shady path and climbs to the D907 (**1h10min**).

Cross the road to the CAMPING VERT sign. Ignore the track between the two stone pillars, but climb the grassy track at the right of it. *(The Short walk begins here.)* Within 10 minutes you clear the chestnuts and find yourself on top of a ridge. As you head southeast on what was once the old road between La Salvetat and St-Pons, the hamlet of Lizarne is seen to the left across the valley, and the farm of La Fourbedié lies below, set like a gem in the midst of tree-darkened slopes. Below it you may notice the scattered remains of the priory of St-Aulary. A flower-bedecked KNOLL (**1h30min**) affords fine views to St-Pons. When a track comes in from the right (**1h45min**), keep left towards a tall shooting hide that would not be out of place in a WWII prisoner-of-war film. Then take the first right, down a grassy

track, leaving the tall hide off to the left (▐ with a *boar* again here, also ▐: ST-PONS 2,5KM). Ignore a track off right two minutes later. Walk round the barrier seen ahead (▐), then pass another tall hide on the left. Beyond a slight rise, the track narrows to a shady path. Descending below holm oaks, you pass to the right of an old RUINED HUT and walk under POWER LINES. A wide path comes in from the left behind you, you pass an IRON CROSS on the left, and come immediately to a T-junction (**2h05min**). Turn left (boars ▐ left and right). In three minutes you pass a large STONE HUT *(capitelle)* on the right; you are now on a jeep track. At a fork (where there is a CYPRESS HEDGE on the left; **2h15min**), go right downhill following BLUE FLASH waymarks. Two minutes later, at a T-junction, turn right (SP is painted in blue on a wall). When you meet a T-junction with a concreted lane (**2h30min**), go left (YELLOW ARROW). This is the **Chemin de Cousteau**. At the next T-junction, go left and then immediately right, on **Rue de Cousteau**. You pass above the well-restored MARKET and come back down to the main road. Turn right past the CATHEDRAL to the **Place Forail** (**2h40min**).

Walk 27: GORGES DE L'ARNETTE AND HAUTPOUL

Distance: 9km/5.6mi; 3h40min
Grade: moderate, with ascents/descents of 360m/1180ft overall. Good surfaces underfoot, but some stretches can be slippery in wet conditions. Green and white PR, red and white GR waymarking. *IGN map 3142 E*
Equipment: see page 55; refreshments available at Hautpoul
How to get there: 🚌 to Moulin Maurel (Car tours 9, 10). Park by the roadside. Or 🚐 or 🚐 to Mazamet (follow purple lines on the map to join the walk just north of the chapel of St-Sauveur)
Longer walk: Moulin Maurel — St-Pierre-d'Esplos — Hautpoul — Brettes — Moulin Maurel. 16km/10mi; 5h20min. Fairly strenuous, with ascents/descents of 500m/1640ft overall. From Moulin Maurel walk south along the D54 past the junction with the ROAD TO PIC DE NORE. Some 150m/yds past this junction you approach a STONE WALL on the right. Leave the road just *before* this wall, taking the clear footpath on your right, descending straight into the gorge. *Take care* on this path (you only follow it for a minute or two, but it is very narrow, and the drop to the right is precipitous). The path takes you to a BRIDGE. Cross the **Arnette River** and then climb a narrow tarmac lane. When you come to a fork, ignore the grassy trail ahead; go left, to climb above a large mill down on the road. Pass a stream to the right, go through a makeshift gate, then climb through chestnuts, oaks, and beech. On reaching a farm (**Les Cousteilles**; **50min**), curl up right between the buildings and leave the farm, passing a large GARAGE/BARN on right. Ignore the grassy track off to the right just past the farm; keep straight ahead uphill on a lane. Then ignore another grassy track into a field; keep climbing under aromatic pines.

When you come to the drab chapel of **St-Pierre-d'Esplos** (**1h**) on the left, with its large cemetery, curve to the right on the road, leaving the chapel off to your left. After 200m/yds, by a CONCRETE CROSS, fork right up a slight incline (☛: HAUTPOUL, MAZAMET). Come to another fork, where there is an IRON CROSS: go right. Your route is now a signposted *Sentier botanique* (and the GR7). Start the descent, with fields sweeping away to the left. When you come to a three-way fork (about five minutes downhill), ignore the track off left into fields *and* the motorable track straight ahead; take the middle track (half-left downhill). In a minute or so *again* take the middle fork. This is still the *Sentier botanique*, but it's as stony as a river bed. Soon come to a well-placed bench looking out across a valley leading into the Arnette. Beyond the bench, at a T-junction, head left downhill. When you come to a crossing track, go straight over and downhill on a footpath. Two minutes later (by a shed on the right with a *Chasse Privée* sign), continue straight ahead on a track, to a junction with a tarmac road, where you turn right downhill, to **Hautpoul** (**1h40min**). Now pick up the main walk at the 55min-point and follow it to the end.

T he ancient fortified village of Hautpoul, a Cathar strong-hold (see box page 49) destroyed in 1212, and the bounding Arnette River are the highlights of this circuit — a fascinating introduction to the ecclesiastical and industrial history of the Montagne Noire.

Start out at the signpost for the hamlet of **Moulin Maurel**. Cross the **Arnette River** on the more southerly of the two bridges (GREEN/WHITE WAYMARKS), pass a WASH HOUSE on the right and, after a garage on the right, go right up a steep tarred lane. This reduces to steps and then a narrow shady path. You rise quickly, with fine views over the Arnette. Beyond a stile, at a T-junction with a path, turn right, soon passing an arrow pointing to HAUTPOUL. The red roofs of the Arnette factories shine up through the trees, and the river gurgles noisily below on the right. 'Waterfalls' of grass spill down the banks of this luxuriant path.

When Hautpoul becomes visible up to the left, *ignore* a path to the left and come to a road. Cross it and, just opposite, take steps down towards the river. Now on a cobbled trail, you pass a humourous wooden sculpture on the left and come onto a gravel track. At the right is a RESTORED MILL, now an artisans' workshop for wooden toys. On the left is the **Arboretum d'Hautpoul** (**30min**), a delightful place for a picnic. From here the track contours above the river to a junction by a WEIR and a MILL IN RUINS. Take the track to the left, then leave it immediately, heading half-left on a path (⌐: HAUTPOUL, GR WAYMARKS). Before long, cobbles come underfoot: this is the old salt route between Narbonne and the Montagne Noire. The deep zigzags minimise the ascent to **Hautpoul** (**55min**), where a statue of the Virgin rises on the site of the old castle, destroyed by Simon de Montfort after a seige lasting four days. Wander through the archways and past the old façades and beautiful doorways. A balcony viewpoint overlooks the houses snuggled below the Virgin's rock and the

Arnette Valley — from where you can hear the delightful sound of rushing water. After your visit, return the way you came, being sure not to miss the overgrown ruins of the Romanesque church of St-Pierre (straight ahead as you descend past a shop on the left selling wooden toys and drinks). Go through an arch at the end of the village, then turn left down steps leading back into the old salt

Old mills in the Arnette Valley. In the 18th century the nascent textile industry was cradled here, and wool was washed in the river. With the coming of the machine age, the industry grew so rapidly that a new town had to be built — Mazamet. But the Arnette was still critical to its success: its waters now supplied the necessary electricity.

Alley in Hautpoul (left) and the old salt trail (far left)

The Arnette Valley below Brettes farm (right) and view from the Croix de Prat (far right)

route. Following the GR way-marks, you pass a tiny CEMETERY on the right.

Back at the junction by the RUINED MILL (**1h30min**, having allowed 15 minutes to walk around Hautpoul), cross the river and meet the D54 at **Moulin de l'Oule**. Now climb the tarmac lane opposite (more GR and green and white waymarks). About 200m/yds uphill, just after passing a few houses, fork left on a signposted footpath to the ruins of **St-Sauveur** (**1h45min**), the Cathar church which fell along with the rest of Hautpoul in 1212. It looks out south to the Virgin on the far side of the Arnette and north to Mazamet.

On the return from St-Sauveur, as you approach the lane, ignore the steps half-left (☛: GR36, MAZA-MET). *(But those travelling by bus or train will use this lower part of the old salt route to get to the main walk.)* Continue on the lane (☛: CROIX DE PRAT). Then, about 50m/yds past the path to the chapel, fork right uphill on a dirt track. This narrows to a path through a mixed wood — mostly chestnut. As it traverses northeast, *watch carefully* for your turn-off sharp right after about 800m/0.5mi *(if you come to a Υ-fork, and the path is descending, you have gone*

114

too far). Turn up sharp right, cross another path, and begin the *real* climb. Keep right at a Y-fork 20 minutes up and go straight over a large junction a minute later. At the next Y-fork, the paths rejoin. It's a steep climb to the **Croix de Prat** (**2h30min**), but the view of Hautpoul, Mazamet and the north is magnificent.

From the cross the green and white waymarks point left, but we take the path straight ahead, at the *right* of the cross (not way-marked). It rises to a T-of paths, where you turn left downhill. In five minutes you emerge on a track and turn right (GR36, green and white waymarks). Now ignore any paths or tracks off this well-waymarked track. Passing under oaks you come to the farm of **Brettes** (**3h**), where you join the GR7. Follow waymarks to circle round the buildings, onto a footpath at the right of a field. The gorgeous Arnette Valley opens up below you, all too briefly. Coming into a forest, zigzag downhill through holly and conifers on a beautiful old trail.

You drop down to the D54 by a large WORKING MILL, where wool is washed and defatted (**3h30min**). Turn left to follow the road beside the river, back to flower-filled **Moulin Maurel** (**3h40min**).

Walk 28: CANAL DU MIDI — CARCASSONNE TO TREBES

See also photograph page 45
Distance: 14km/8.7mi; 4h10min
Grade: very easy. Red and white GR waymarking at the start, then no waymarking. *IGN map 2345 E*
Equipment: see page 55; no refreshments available between Carcassonne and Trèbes
How to get there: 🚗 to La Cité (Porte Narbonnaise; Car tours 9-

11). Or 🚌 or 🚆 to Carcassonne, from where you can start the walk at the bridge over the Aude. Return by 🚌, 🚆 or taxi from Trèbes to Carcassonne
Short walk: Trèbes — Ecluse de Villedubert — Trèbes. 8km/5mi; 2h. 🚗 to Trèbes (Car tour 10); park near the canal. Walk to the Villedubert Lock and back.

The Canal du Midi, one of the most evocative images of the south of France, was created by the ingenuity of one man and the labour of 12,000. Among the obstacles to be overcome was a 174m/570ft-high ridge west of Carcassonne. Paul Riquel, a wealthy tax collector, had the solution: bring in water for the locks from the rushing streams of the Montagne Noire. He even put up a third of the money himself, sacrificing his daughters' dowries. Sadly, he died in 1680 — six months before the canal was opened. With the building of the adjacent Canal Latéral à la Garonne in the 19th century, the link to the Atlantic was complete, fulfilling a dream dating back to Roman times.

Start out at the **Porte Narbonnaise**, the main gate to La Cité. With your back to the gate, walk left downhill on the road (GR36), keeping the large CAR PARK on your right. In two minutes fork left up a path (GR waymark on a lamp post), to skirt the walls of the citadel. Two minutes later come to a tarmac lane and go left uphill into a square. Walk to the front of

the church (**St-Gimer**), cross the road to the *boulangerie*, and turn right. Go straight over a crossroads; you approach a BRIDGE and a PARK. Cross another road and go through the park. Turn right under the bridge in the park (**Pont Vieux**) and then head left down to the track beside the Aude. Turn right on the track and walk under the main N113 road bridge (**Pont**

The fairy-tale towers of La Cité (see also page 45)

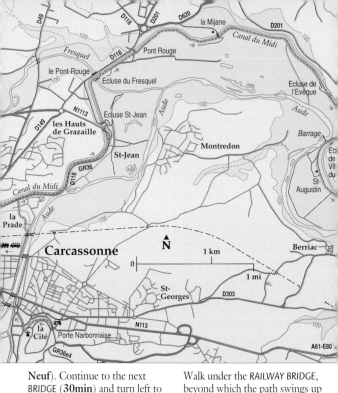

Neuf). Continue to the next *BRIDGE* (**30min**) and turn left to cross it. On the far side, swing right, back down to the river.

Walk under the *RAILWAY BRIDGE*, beyond which the path swings up left. Cross a lane and go straight up a road (GR waymark on a lamp

The canal can be utterly tranquil or bustling with activity.

(D118; you will hear the traffic). Cross the road, drop down to the TOWPATH (**45min**), and turn right. For the next few hours you will amble beside this delightful waterway, cheering on the rented holiday barges as they navigate the short elliptical locks.

At at the **Ecluse St-Jean** (**1h 05min**), you part company with the GR. Continuing to the echo of bird song, you reach a bridge at **La Mijane** (**1h50min**); this is the halfway point along the canal. At the **Ecluse de Villedubert** (**3h10min**), Villedubert can be seen across the lock, shaded by palm trees and cypresses. Here you have to leave the canal, but keep along a track going in the same direction; the Aude, and a weir, are just on your right. Continue ahead, at the left-hand side of a quarry, on a track running above the canal. In five minutes you pass the houses of **St-Augustin** and five minutes later rejoin the canal. On coming into **Trèbes**, where there are picnic tables on the far side of the canal, you approach a bridge. Don't cross it; turn right in front of it, following CARCAS-SONNE. Soon you will pass a BAR on your right (**4h10min**), where you can have a drink and telephone for a taxi. Or, to get to the railway station and bus stops, cross the Aude and continue along the D610 for another 0.5km/10 minutes. (A circular walk, returning along the Aude, would have been ideal, but is not possible; there is nowhere to cross the river between Trèbes and Carcassonne.)

post on the right). You climb through a housing estate (**La Prade**); at the first opportunity, turn up right to the main road

117

Walk 29: MINERVE

Distance: 5km/3mi; 2h
Grade: *fairly easy ascents/descents of 200m/650ft overall; agility required in some places. Sparse yellow waymarking. No shade.*
IGN map 2445 E
Equipment: see page 55; refreshments available in Minerve

How to get there: 🚌 to Minerve. From St-Pons-de-Thomières (Car tour 10) take the D907 south for 25km, then turn right on the D10e and right again on the D10, following MINERVE. Park on the D10 just before the village (paid car park).

The site of Minerve, astride a rock buttress at the confluence of the Brian and Cesse gorges, has been inhabited since prehistoric times. Its fame, however, derives from one of the most brutal battles in the Albigensian wars (see box page 49): in 1210 Simon de Montfort laid siege for seven weeks until his catapults destroyed the Cathars' water supply and the people were forced to capitulate. They were given the choice of surrender or death; 180 chose death by pyre.

Start the walk at the CAR PARK on the D10. Cross the bridge into **Minerve** and walk to the top of the village. Head left towards the spiky tower of the old château. Walk to the right of the tower, then descend a stone-laid path on the right (just past a small vegetable garden; there is a GR 'X' on this path). The path curls down into the **Brian Gorge**, then levels out and turns back to the right (south) to circle below the village (the '**Chemin de Ronde**'; **15min**; YELLOW WAYMARKS). As it again curls right to head west, you'll see a replica of *La Malvoisine* on the far side of the gorge — the most feared of all de Montfort's catapults, as it was just across the gorge from the water supply. Cross the footbridge on the left now, just at the confluence of the **Brian** and **Cesse**. Then take steep steps up the far side to a cart track, the **Chemin de l'Estrade**. Turn left here, passing to the right of **La Malvoisine**. The views from this plateau, into the Brian Gorge and over to Minerve, are superb. At a THREE-WAY FORK (**30min**), take the cart track to the left, ignoring the surfaced track ahead (your return route) and a path to the right. You skirt the edge of the

cliffs above the Brian, with good views back to the Chemin de Ronde. There are vineyards on the right, and you will follow these to the top of the climb. When a cart track comes in from half-right, keep ahead towards a house. Pass just to the left of the house (**La Courounelle**; **1h02min**) and keep ahead (there is an ORANGE FLASH on a telephone pole at the right). At a fork two minutes later, keep right on the main track (YELLOW FLASH, CAIRN). From here there is a good view down over the Cesse Valley and La Caumette. Ignore a track coming in from the left in two minutes; walk ahead on the motorable track.

You pass to the left of the few houses of **Padene** (**1h15min**), where tar comes underfoot. The small Goury Gorge is on your left and vineyards on the right. Keep to the road, rising through **Mayranne**. At the exit from this hamlet, don't go downhill left on the road, take the dirt track straight ahead, rising slightly. When the way levels out, ignore a track off right to a farm and then a cart track off right. You can see the D10 down to the left, on the far side of the Cesse. When the track curls left

118

The Brian Gorge

(**1h32min**), turn right into a wide fire-break but, after 15m/yds, descend half-left on a minor cart track *(no waymarks)*. Minerve is on your left now. The track descends quickly to an abandoned vineyard (overgrown with bright-blooming wild flowers in spring). Walk round or across the field, then make a U-turn to head back the way you came, so that Minerve is on your *right* and *La Malvoisine* is ahead of you. Making straight for the catapult, you come onto a track at the edge of cultivated vineyards: follow it straight ahead, back to the three-way fork first encountered at the 30min-point. Back at **La Malvoisine** (**1h 40min**), retrace your steps to cross the FOOTBRIDGE (noticing some enticing grassy paths down to the Brian as you go) and rise back to the **Chemin de Ronde**. Turn left to continue the circuit, passing the covered walkway leading to the Cathars' water supply (**Chemin Couvert**) and the well itself (**Puits de St-Rustique**). The Chemin de Ronde continues as a track

The tower of the old château (left) and La Malvoisine (right), a replica of the catapult responsible for the destruction of Minerve's water supply in 1210

running just above the **river Cesse**, past caves. Ignore steps up right to the Poterne Sud (the south keep) and continue straight ahead on asphalt. On the left, just before the modern road bridge, is one of two rock tunnels (PONT NATUREL), where the Cesse carved its way through the limestone (in summer, when the water is low, you can walk through it). Pass the road down to the cemetery and head up the road towards the village. At the T-junction turn sharp right, cross the bridge, and return to the CAR PARK (**2h**).

119

Walk 30: CIRCUIT ABOVE LAGRASSE

marking. *IGN map 2446 O*

Equipment: see page 55; refreshments available in Lagrasse

How to get there: 🚌 to Lagrasse (Car tour 11)

Short walk: Montagne de la Côte. 3.5km/2.2mi; 1h35min. Fairly easy, with ascents/descents of 210m/670ft overall. Follow the main walk to the 1h10min-point. Turn right here, just *before* the notice board, then turn right again. After about 200m/yds, go left on a path between stone walls. You rise 50m/165ft, cross the crest of this mini-mountain, and then descend (keep left 400m/yds downhill at a fork) to a track. Turn right here and pick up the main walk again at the 2h15min-point.

Distance: 6km/3.7mi; 2h25min

Grade: fairly easy ascent/descent of 160m/525ft. Yellow PR way-

There is some evidence that the Abbey of Lagrasse was founded in 799 by the Emperor Charlemagne. True or not, the area abounds with place names referring to him. While the 'high point' of the walk — literally and figuratively — is the view from the Roc de Cagalière, you will also come across 'Charlemagne's Foot' and look out to 'Charlemagne's Buttocks'!

Start out at the SCHOOL on the main D3 in **Lagrasse**, walking south towards RIBAUTE. Pass the D212 to Ribaute on the left, and 50 paces further on turn left on a concrete lane (sign on the left: SENTIER D'EMILIE, LE PIED DE CHARLEMAGNE). Ignore all turn-offs as you rise, with a fine view back to the abbey.

Just past a HEDGE OF CYPRESS TREES on the left, at a three-way

Lagrasse from the Roc Cagalière. Les Fesses de Charlemagne (see box opposite) are visible on the hillside to the left of the abbey tower.

Le Pied de Charlemagne: according to legend, this is the hoof-print of Charlemagne's horse. The emperor was returning from a successful campaign against the Saracens when his mount made a false step. Despite his undoubted horsemanship, the emperor was flung clear across the valley, where his ample buttocks (fesses) left their imprint on the hillside (the rounded green slopes with an indentation of scree down the middle in the photograph opposite).

junction, take the middle route. Three minutes later, just after this eroded track makes a U-bend to the right, turn left up a footpath (**15min**; waymark and CAIRN). This lovely path rises gently northeast through pines towards the Roc de Cagalière. This was the old trail between Lagrasse and Tournissan, and you will sometimes see cobbles underfoot.

At a Y-fork, turn left, passing a small field on the right. A path takes you the short way up to the top of the **Roc de Cagalière** (**35min**), the perfect viewpoint down over Lagrasse, north to the Montagne d'Alaric, and south over the rolling hills of the Corbières. If the wind is in the right direction, the Pyrenees will emerge from the haze.

Return from this rock promontory the way you came, with the little field now on your left. Back at the fork beyond it, turn sharp left, passing another field on the left. When you meet a forestry track, turn left and follow it round a hairpin bend to the right, contouring through pines. While there are no views now, this track on the eastern flanks of the miniature **Montagne de la Côte** is a delight of wild flowers in spring. Some 600m/yds along the track, watch on the right for a path marked with two CAIRNS and follow it 50m/yds (past a small field on the right) to another, small rock outcrop with a large circular hole — the **Pied de Charlemagne** (**50min**; photograph above). There is a path from here directly down to Lagrasse, but we haven't tried it.

Return to the forestry track and continue to the right. As a track comes in from behind you to the left (from Ribaute), you come to a junction with a GREEN WATER TANK and WALKERS' INFORMATION PANEL (both on the right; **1h10min**). (*The Short walk turns right here.*) Walk past the tank and, after 30m/yds, turn left on the **Sentier botanique** and follow its meanderings until you regain the forestry track further south. The colour of the track underfoot changes to deep iron-rich red soil and you reach the **Col Rouch** (Red Pass; **1h35min**). (Another legend has it that the soil is stained red with the blood of martyred Cathars.) Ignore the track straight ahead here; curve to the right, then turn right off the main track (quickly passing a ⊺: SENTIER PEDESTRE).

From this track there is a superb view down left over the vineyards of La Peyrouse and north towards Lagrasse and the abbey, with Charlemagne's Buttocks above to the left and Alaric rising in the background. Ignore both a cairned path on the right (**2h15min**; the Short walk descent) and, just over 150m/yds further on, the path you ascended at the start. Retracing your outward route, you come back to the SCHOOL in **Lagrasse** (**2h25min**).

121

Walk 31: CIRCUIT ABOVE TERMES

See also photograph page 51
Distance: 8km/5mi; 2h45min
Grade: easy-moderate, with ascents/descents of about 300m/1000ft overall; ample shade. Red and white GR, yellow PR waymarking. *IGN map 2447 OT*
Equipment: see page 55; nearest refreshments: Lagrasse (12km)
How to get there: 🚌 to Termes (Car tour 11); park at the roadside near the entrance to the château (there is also a car park further east)

Short walks/picnic suggestions:
1 Watercourse. Up to 50min. Easy; follow the main walk to the 15min- or 25min-point and back.
2 Serre Laitière. 1h15min. Easy ascent/descent of 160m/525ft. Walk to the château and continue uphill past it, to Serre Laitière.

Without doubt our favourite walk in the Corbières, this ramble is extremely varied and beautiful. You start out along a gurgling watercourse, climb to a flower-filled plateau and descend past an idyllic farm to the Château de Termes and then to the enchanting village itself.

Start out in **Termes** by crossing the bridge to the château. On the far side, turn left on the CAMIN DEL MOLIN, beside the **river Sou**. After passing behind the MAIRIE, you pick up red and white GR waymarks. You're following an old watercourse that used to supply the mill. Cross a grassy track and continue straight ahead. Then turn right in front of a fenced-in vegetable plot; after a 10-15 paces you meet a much wider watercourse, which you follow to the left, with the murmuring river not far below. The play of light and shade is delightful on this stretch. A DAM (**15min**) marks the start of the waterway. Walk back a few paces from the dam, then turn left up a clear path. It rises quite steeply away from a meander in the river, then drops again; soon the river is jumping down in tiers beside you — a beautiful spot (**25min**). Just over five minutes later the path finally leaves the river, heading southwest through an open grassy area. At a fork some three minutes along, igore the path to the right; continue straight ahead. But at the Y-fork which follows immediately, go right (where the other branch goes down to the river). At this point you may notice a distinctive rock pillar ahead — the **Roc de Femme Prenz** (Pregnant Woman). We've reached the bed of the **Nougairole Stream** (**35min**): hop across it (there's little water) and continue on the path on the far side, climbing towards the Roc de Femme Prenz through the **Forêt Domaniale de Termes**, a mixed woodland where oak and beech predominate. Watch for a path on your left and turn downhill to a VIEWPOINT (**1h**) over the **Sou Gorge** and the waterfall that feeds it.

Then return to the main path which quickly crosses a natural rock 'bridge' (**Pont de la Caune**) above an enormous CAVE on the right. Although this section is very narrow (about 1.5m/4ft wide), it is just 4m/12ft long and would only be potentially dangerous in *very* strong winds.

As you contour now at the foot of the **Nitable Roc** buttress, there are open views due south to the table-topped Montagne de Tauch with its relay. The path dips, then quickly rises to the TOP OF THE PLATEAU (**1h25min**). In case of mist, *watch carefully for the GR and PR waymarks here*, but on clear days the main path through the

Right: Roc de Femme Prenz (Pregnant Woman Rock), one of the landmarks on the walk. Below: the idyllic Bergerie de Serre Laitière (top), view back to the Château de Termes on the descent into the village (middle) and the dam at the source of the watercourse that once fed the mill at Termes but is now used for irrigation.

flower-filled *garrigues* is easily seen. Up here you're on top of the world, with open views to the Pech de Bugarach and the Pyrenees. Descending from the plateau, the path heads northwest, with the Caulière Valley below to the left. *Again, watch the waymarks carefully on this stretch,* as the path zigzags (at the first of these *lacets,* a path contours ahead, but you must turn *sharply back to the left.*) About five minutes after entering a beautiful oak wood, *again take care:* at a fork, where the GR goes sharp left, keep *straight ahead* on a contouring path (YELLOW FLASH). Ten minutes later come to the idyllic **Bergerie de Serre Laitière** (**2h10min**), from where you follow a contouring track to the foot of the **Château de Termes** (**2h35min**). Continue down to **Termes** (**2h45min**).

Walk 32: PEYREPERTUSE AND THE FONTAINE DE LA JACQUETTE

See map pages 126-127; see also photograph page 49

Distance: 4.5km/ 2.8mi; 2h15min

Grade: strenuous ascent/descent of 330m/ 1100ft; ample shade. The paths are very slippery when wet. You must be sure-footed and have a head for heights. Yellow PR, red and white GR waymarking. *IGN map 2447 OT*

Equipment: see page 55; walking stick(s). Refreshments available at nearby Rouffiac

How to get there: 🚗 to the Col de Grès (Car tour 11); alternatively, start in Rouffiac (see map)

Short walk: Fontaine de la Jacquette. 2.5km/ 1.6mi; 1h20min. Quite strenuous ascent/descent of 150m/490ft, requiring agility. Follow the main walk for 40 minutes, then jump to the 1h35min-point.

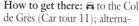

Photograph: the Fontaine de la Jacquette. It was probably built in the 13th century by St-Louis. His mother lost her silver goblet there.

The most famous and extensive of the Cathar châteaux, Peyrepertuse makes for a short but fairly demanding hike. From the site, it seems the world is at your feet. Later in the walk, the rock chaos below the Fontaine de la Jacquette is a veritable rock garden of wild flowers, moss and holm oaks.

Start out at the **Col de Grès**: facing the sign for the col, go right on a grassy track (*YELLOW WAYMARKS*). In three minutes the track bends 90° left and narrows to a path. From here on *watch your maymarks;* there are many twists and turns as the path dips slightly, then begins its steady ascent through pines (**8min**). The only unmarked stretch comes up about 30 minutes uphill (four minutes past a small scree), when the path bends sharp right and rises over a low wall: only after the path bends left again will you find a yellow waymark on a tree.

When you meet the crossing GR (**40min**), which has taken a different route up from the col, turn right uphill and follow the red and white waymarks another 145m/475ft, to the **Château de Peyrepertuse** (**1h10min**). From here the views are magnificent — you look over the Verdouble Valley to Quéribus and Tauch, to Bugarach and the Pyrenees. If you

decide to visit the fortress (see footnote page 50), it will cost you the entrance fee plus another 60m/ 200ft of ascent to the Château St-Georges (not included in the main walk).

Return to the JUNCTION WITH THE PR ROUTE (**1h35min**) and turn right. The path drops steeply to the 13th-century **Fontaine de la Jacquette** (**1h45min**), built when the Peyrepertuse fortifications were being extended.

Beyond here the path drops through a mixed wood and moss-coated rock chaos, crossing a few rock screes. Cairns as well as waymarks guide you on this enchanting but demanding stretch. Beyond the final, long scree (a rock garden of wild flowers), *watch out:* the path bends sharp left.

After you pass a SPRING on the left (**2h05min**) the way widens to a track and descends gently to the **Col de Grès** (in the last 20m/yds joining the GR; **2h15min**). Turn left, back to your car.

Walk 33: CIRCUIT BELOW PEYREPERTUSE

See also photograph page 49
Distance: 4.5km/2.8mi; 2h15min
Grade: easy, with two short ascents (150m/500ft overall). Some of the paths are narrow; some are stony. *Little shade.* Outside summer, when the river is high, it may not be possible to reach the waterfalls shown below. Yellow PR waymarking. *IGN map 2447 OT*
Equipment: see page 55; refreshments available in Duilhac.
How to get there: 🚗 to Duilhac-sous-Peyrepertuse (Car tour 11). Park on the D14 near the *auberge*.

This walk below Peyrepertuse looks up to the château from the south — not the best vantage point. But the best part of the walk in any case is the 'marble' river bed of the Verdouble, with its tiered waterfalls.

Start out on the D14 in **Duilhac**: from the *auberge* walk southeast (towards Quéribus) for about 100m/yds, then turn left down a narrow lane below the village. (If you come to the *boulangerie*, you have gone too far.) You'll soon see yellow flashes. Leaving the gardens behind, the waymarks take you beside a vineyard. Now

The turquoise waters of the tiered cascade in the Verdouble

on a footpath, you walk below and parallel with the road; Peyreper-tuse rises above you to the left. The path rises steeply up to the D14, where you turn right and follow the road for 35m/yds, to the **Col de la Croix Dessus** (**35min**). Go right here on a cart track, following the electricity wires (⛊: *MOULIN DE RIBAUTE*). Now there are good views back to Duilhac, with Peyrepertuse above it. At a U-bend, leave the track and follow the footpath ahead for about 15 minutes, enjoying some glimpses of the vineyards in the Verdouble Valley through foliage. When the stony path at first *seems* to descend, it really climbs up to the left in a tight U-bend, and then descends into the valley. Now the **Verdouble Gorge** opens up on the left, and from the verti-ginous edge of the path, you will have the tremendous view shown on page 125. On reaching a

T-junction with a stony track (**1h**), *go left* (ignoring any yellow 'X'). You come to a concrete embank-ment at the river's edge. On the far side is the the ruined **Moulin de Ribaute**, an old wheat-grinding mill. If you do this walk in high summer, it's likely that you'll find planks in place, allowing you to cross the river here. If not, you should at least be able to cross a ford a short way downstream, to reach the mill and the cascades. From the river return to the junction at the 1h-point and go straight ahead. The track soon narrows to a path. Walk to the right of a first vineyard and then go left, to keep a second vineyard on your right. This shady path is a flutter of butterflies. Watch your footing, however; it is narrow in places, with a hefty drop. Having climbed back to the D14 in **Duilhac** (**2h15min**), turn right, back to the *auberge*.

Walk 34: CIRCUIT TO QUERIBUS

Distance: 8.5km/5.3mi; 2h55min
Grade: moderate, with an ascent/descent of 340m/1115ft. The descent path is very steep in places and requires agility. *No shade;* on sunny days, start out early, when there is some shade from the cliffs. Yellow and orange and yellow and red PR

waymarking. *IGN map 2447 OT*
Equipment: see page 55; walking stick(s). Refreshments available at Cucugnan
How to get there: 🚌 to the eastern entrance to Cucugnan off the D14 (Car tour 11). Park beside the road, near the sign: *CUCUGNAN 0,9KM.*

While the holocaust at Montségur is generally regarded as the last battle in the crusade against the Albigensians (see box page 49), Quéribus continued to provide refuge for a handful of Cathars. In 1255 St-Louis eradicated this final pocket of resistance, but it appears that the castle was taken by trickery, not by armed assault. At that time Quéribus stood on the border between France and Aragon, so its capture greatly strengthened the line of royal fortresses guarding the frontier. Only in 1659, when the border was moved further south, did Quéribus lose its strategic importance.

Start out opposite the sign *CUCUGNAN 0.9KM.* Walk south-west down the lane marked with *RED HORSESHOES* at the outset. After 100m/yds pass a lane off right with red and yellow way-marks (the return route) and come to a FOUNTAIN. Keep straight ahead here, following yellow and orange flashes. At a Y-fork 100m/yds further on, keep left. Walking between vineyards, you cross a stream and go straight ahead on the lane. 350m/yds further on, keep right at two Y-forks in succession, eventually passing a stand of cypresses at **Les Fontainilles** (**20min**). The lane curls back west for a short time (affording a fine view back over Cucugnan and to Peyrepertuse and Bugarach), before resuming its

easterly traverse towards the flat Montagne de Tauch with its relay. When the tar ends at a fork (**45min**), turn half-right up a bulldozed track. Now you have to make your way up this extremely unpleasant track (which *may* be tarred in future) for the next 35 minutes, until you reach a contouring track on the crest. This is the **Sentier Cathare** (**1h20min**), which runs from the Château d'Aguilar to Peyrepertuse, and is waymarked in red and yellow. Soon you have a first view of Quéribus, with the Pyrenees (hopefully snow-capped) behind it. A beautiful ridge is ahead too, rising on the south side of the Cucugnan Valley — the Roque de la Pourcatière. Behind it, to the right, is the silhouette of Bugarach.
From the PARKING AREA for the **Château de Quéribus** (**1h45min**; ticket office, WCs, picnic tables), a path rises another 100m/300ft to the chateau itself. (Add another 1h return, if you take this walk.) The main walk continues by turning right uphill to where the Quéribus

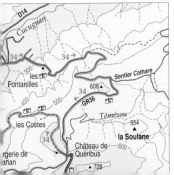

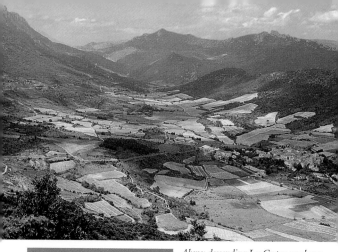

Above: descending Les Costes, you have a fine view over Cucugnan and its valley. The Château de Peyrepertuse is just visible on the ridge behind Cucugnan.
Left: Château de Quéribus

(**2h25min**) the path contours through high grass. At a T-junction with a track, go right. The **Bergerie de Granan** is set up on the left. Making straight for Cucugnan, pass to the right of a house. Some 15 minutes along the track, ignore a track off left and then a track off right. Now walking on a level track between vineyards, you look up right to the cliff you rounded earlier and the ridge traversed by the Sentier Cathare. You quickly meet the bend of a tarred lane: turn left, then follow the lane in a curve to the right (ignoring another lane off to the left). The lane curls right, back towards Tauch (where a cross is visible) and emerges on the lane where the walk began. Turn left, back to the sign CUCUGNAN 0,9KM (**2h55min**).

access road ends (yellow and red flashes, ▶: CUCUGNAN). This is the most beautiful part of the walk, if the most demanding: the path through *maquis* aglow with tiny blue grass lilies (*Aphyllanthes monspeliensis*) rises to a grassy promontory, dips, rises again and then descends *very* steeply down the shoulder of **Les Costes** (keep right at a Y-fork a short way down). The views — back to Quéribus and the Pyrenees, over to Peyrepertuse, the Roque de la Pourcatière and Bugarach, and down to the Cucugnan and Verdouble valleys are simply magnificent.

Once down in the valley

Walk 35: CIRCUIT ABOVE TUCHAN

Distance: 6km/3.7mi; 2h25min
Grade: moderate, with ascents
and descents of 300m/980ft overall; *little shade*. You must be agile:
the descent path from the chapel is
slippery when wet and it may be a
problem to cross the Ruisseau de
Faste outside high summer. Since
this crossing is near the *end* of the
walk, you may prefer to start at the
chapel: if so, from Tuchan take the
little road above the wine
cooperative signposted to Mont
Tauch and Notre-Dame-de-Faste,
and begin at the 1h35min-point
— or do the walk in the reverse
direction. Yellow PR waymarking.
IGN map 2447 OT
Equipment: see page 55; long
trousers, walking stick(s). Refreshments available at nearby Tuchan

How to get there: 🚗 to Ségure
(detour on Car tour 11). From
Padern drive to Tuchan and, in the
centre of the village, take the D39
signposted PRODUCTEURS DE
MONT TAUCH (Palairac road).

The Château of Ségure and the chapel of Notre-Dame-de-
Faste are the highlights of this gorgeous walk in the foothills of the Montagne de Tauch, but you'll also see a hamlet
bursting with roses and … an angora goat farm!

Start out at the pretty, partly-
abandoned hamlet of **Ségure**: take
the cart track just south of the
houses and little bridge (⚑: NOTRE-
DAME-DE-FASTE). You're heading
towards the Montagne de Tauch.
Turn right on another track
(**5min**; waymarked), and then go
sharp left immediately. At a fork
two minutes later (where there is a
solitary house on the left), go
steeply left uphill on a narrow
eroded path. The path bends 90°
left, above the house, and levels
out amidst a plethora of *Lavandula
stoechas* and white Montpellier
cistus. Tauch is on your left now,
and you can see the chapel of
Notre-Dame-de-Faste above. Soon
the castle, your first goal, comes
into view on the right, and you
approach it on a very pretty grassy
path, full of broom and junipers.
When you come onto a cart track,
follow it to the right, to a grassy
area with cypresses. Now three

tracks are ahead: ignore the gravel
track to the left (your ongoing
route), the grassy track ahead *and*
the track to the right (to a house
belonging to the 'Château de
Ségure' vineyards). Take the
footpath between the two tracks, to
rise to the ruins of the **Château de
Ségure** (**25min**). This is a lovely
spot for a picnic.
Return from the château and turn
hard right on the gravel track
(with the sign CHATEAU DE SEGURE
on your right). Follow this downhill below the ruins but, after only
50 paces, turn hard left on a grassy
path, descending below the
cypresses in the parking area. At a
fork 15 minutes along, keep right
on a track and, two minutes later,
at a Y-fork, go right on an eroded
path. Strawberry trees enliven this
stretch, but it is a hefty climb and
very tiring in heat. Finally the path
levels out in a grassy area amidst a
myriad of wild flowers.

129

Ségure (above) and Notre-Dame-de-Faste (left). Legends has it that the chapel was founded by sailors in peril, who were only saved by seeing a light atop the Montagne de Tauch, although the ceremonial use of the site, with its nearby spring, probably dates back to pagan times. On the way to the chapel you pass a farm breeding angora goats.

At a farm (LE MOHAIR DU TAUCH; **1h25min**), where you'll see long-haired angora goats, you come to a gravel track. Enjoying a fine view back to the ruined castle and over vineyards, follow the track downhill to the chapel of **Notre-Dame-de-Faste** (**1h35min**). (Water is available at the picnic area 150m down the access road). To return to Ségure, walk to the right of the main door, then turn right down a steep path at the east

end of the chapel. *Watch the waymarks carefully throughout the zigzag descent.* When you approach the **Ruisseau de Faste** (**1h45min**) you may find that the footbridges are washed away. If so, you'll have to scramble 1.5m/4ft down into a messy, muddy gully and over to the right-hand side of the stream. Two minutes later you have to repeat the exercise, to get back to the left-hand side (where the path ahead is marked with an 'X'): this is best done by turning a short way left upstream, where the drop is less (again 1.5m/4ft).

After regaining the left-hand side of the stream, a VINEYARD will be on your right. At a T-junction with a motorable track (**2h05min**) turn right, then curve left with the track, ignoring the minor track on the right. The track heads between vineyards, then keeps just beside the right-hand side of the river. When you reach the D39, follow it to the left for 350m/yds, back to **Ségure** (**2h25min**).

Walk 36: THE 'ROMAN' BRIDGE AT BUGARACH

Distance: 4.5km/2.8mi; 1h40min
Grade: easy-moderate, with ascents/descents of 130m/425ft overall, but agility is required; some of the paths are steep and narrow, slippery when wet. Yellow PR waymarks. *IGN map 2347 OT*
Equipment: see page 55; refreshments available in Bugarach
How to get there: 🚌 to Bugarach (Car tour 11); park near the Mairie.

Short walk/picnic suggestion: Pont Romain (2km/1.2mi; 30min). Park by the transformer on the D14, just over 2km west of Bugarach village. Follow the walk from the 32min-point to the bridge and return the same way.
Alternative walk: Pech de Bugarach. 6km/3.7mi; 2h45min. Strenuous ascent/descent of 560m/1850ft. You must be sure-footed and have a head for heights (only recommended for experienced walkers). *Do not attempt the ascent after rain or in strong winds!* The path begins at the Col du Linas, on the D14 east of Bugarach village.

Autumn 1992 brought terrible storms to southwestern France. Swollen rivers swept away several Roman bridges (including the single-arched span at Vaison-la-Romaine). The people of Bugarach lost their Roman bridge too, but the following year local stonemasons donated their time and talents to create an exact replica. Yet however pretty the little gorge and the new 'Roman' bridge, the superb views over to Bugarach provide the highlight of this walk.

Start the walk at the MAIRIE on the D14 in **Bugarach**. Turn right down a track on the west side of the building (☞: SENTIER D'EMILIE, LE PONT ROMAIN). After crossing a little bridge, walk to the left of a cinder-brick wall on a farm track. Bugarach rises to the left, while you cross the grassy fields surrounding Bugarach village. When the track curves right, there is an especially fine view to the peak. On coming to the D14 again (**20min**), follow it to the left for 1km/0.6mi, until you come to an electricity TRANSFORMER. Turn right here, through an old gravel quarry (**32min**; ☞: PONT ROMAIN). At a Y-fork, where the main track goes left, keep ahead on a grassy track. A CATTLE ENCLOSURE is on the left. The way narrows to a path and turns left, still beside the enclosure.

You rejoin the main track just at the start of the descent: turn right. In five minutes you're down at the new **'Pont Romain'** (**45min**), where a plaque pays tribute to the eight stonemasons who recreated the original bridge. The setting, a tiny gorge along the **Blanque**

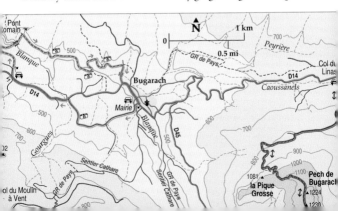

Bugarach's new 'Roman' bridge over the Blanque Stream, built in 1993

Stream, with rock pools and an old stone-laid path, is exquisite. To continue the walk, climb the steep footpath to the right. At a T-junction (**50min**), turn right (↑: BUGARACH). (The way to the left is another waymarked walk, to La Vialasse). Through the clearings in the *garrigues* there are wonderful views down to the right over the Blanque Valley and east to Bugarach.

At a CLEARING from where you have the *best* view of the mountain (**1h05min**), be sure to turn steeply left downhill (where the main path *appears* to go straight on). Steps cut into the rock help you down this eroded, fairly narrow path. *Watch the way-marking — there are several zigzags!* The path climbs again, heading north via a couple of *lacets* to the left, where you may need to use hands and feet for short stretches. Finally, at the top of the climb (**1h25min**) you clear the trees and look down over the fields at the start of the walk and ahead to the Bugarach.

Coming on to an old stony track a couple of minutes later, you enjoy pretty glimpses of Bugarach village as you descend. Pass by a few houses, then follow a lane over a bridge and past a house on the left with an exquisite garden. When you reach the D14 (**1h35min**), follow it to the left, back to the MAIRIE in **Bugarach** (**1h40min**).

The Pech de Bugarac, surrounded by a collar of grassy fields, is the focal point on this walk. The highest peak in the Corbières, this monolith of intriguing rock forms is best appreciated from the west, near Bugarach village.

GLOSSARY

Bartizan: overhanging, battlemented corner turret (of a castle)

Baume: shelter beneath rock

Belvédère: elevated viewpoint

Bergerie: shelter for animals (and shepherds)

Borie: small drystone building, usually with a domed roof (photo page 64)

Buvette: snack bar

Camelle: pile of salt near salt pans

Capitelle: as borie

Castelas, castellas, castellaras: old ruined castle (photograph page 102)

Cathars: See box page 49.

Cause: vast limestone plateau, where most rainfall quickly seeps through the porous rock

Chasse privée: private hunting ground

Cirque: a valley ending in a deep rounded 'amphitheatre' of rock (photograph pages 40-41)

Cité: old term used for a grouping of citizens (as Lavène, Walk 16); also the oldest part of a city (as La Cité at Carcassonne)

Clos: enclosed parcel of cultivated land (photograph page 34)

Col: pass

Dégustation: wine-tasting

Dolmen: prehistoric sepulchral chamber of standing stones supporting a flattish stone 'roof'

Dolomitic rock: rock composed of soluble calcium and less soluble magnesium. The calcium erodes more quickly under the action of rainwater and streams, giving rise to weird formations, for which the French have a very apt name (*ruiniform*).

Domaine: estate (vineyard)

Garrigue, maquis: terrain resulting from the degradation of the Mediterranean forest (through fires or grazing), differentiated by the nature of their soil and characteristic flora. The *garrigue* is an open limestone wasteland on non-acidic soil, with small pockets of vegetation. Typical plants include Aleppo pines, kermes oak, holm oak, box, thistles, gorse, rough grass and wild aromatic plants like lavender, thyme and rosemary. The *maquis* is a dense covering of evergreen plants growing on acidic soil, usually with small hairy or leathery leaves to help withstand the dry conditions. Flora include trees like cork and holm oaks, junipers, box, strawberry trees and myrtle, as well as smaller bushes like rosemary, jerusalem sage, broom, heather, and *Cistus*. Larger trees like chestnuts and maritime pines may also be present.

Garrigues, Les: an area north of Nimes, described in Car tour 7, which exhibits the features of the *garrigue*

Gouffre: gulf, abyss

GR (Grande Randonnée): long-distance footpath, waymarked with red and white paint flashes; see page 56.

Grotte: cave

Lavogne: stone-paved basin for watering livestock (photograph page 90)

Manade: raising of bulls or horses in the Camargue

Maquis: see *Garrigue*

Maquis, The: French Resistance during World War II

Mas: country house, usually applied to a farm

Massif: mountain mass with various peaks

Menhir: ancient megalithic standing stone

Oppidum: defensive position of drystone walls at vantage points. The Ligurians built the first *oppida*.

PR (Petite Randonnée): local waymarked walk, fairly short, often circular; see page 56.

Resurgence: the reappearance above ground of a subterranean watercourse; for example, the Fontaine-de-Vaucluse (photograph page 22)

Rive droite, rive gauche: right bank, left bank of a river. (The banks of a river are defined *from* the source.)

Rocher: rock

Ruffes: eroded limestone slopes with a high red clay content, as at Salagou (photograph page 102).

Ruiniform: a chaos of dolomitic rock which has eroded into the shape of ruins. The rocks may look like a building or even a whole town, or sometimes a ruined sculpture. Montpellier-le-Vieux (Walk 19) and the Cirque de Mourèze (Walk 23, are textbook examples.

Sentier (botanique): footpath. (A *sentier botanique* usually is accompanied by information panels describing the botany and geology of a specific area; see, for example, Walk 5.)

Table d'orientation: panoramic viewpoint, usually with a circular stone 'table' marked with the points of the compass and pinpointing the location of towns, mountains, etc.

Via: road. By 100BC Rome held much of the land between the Alps and the Pyrenees. Their most important highways were the *Via Agrippa* via Orange and Avignon to Arles, the *Via Aurelia* via Nice, Fréjus, Aix and Nimes to Arles and then Spain (today the N7 follows much the same route), and the *Via Domitia* via Sisteron, Apt and Pont Julien south to the *Via Aurelia*.

Index

Geographical names comprises the only entries in this Index; for non-geographical names, see Contents, page 3. A page number in *italic type* indicates a map; a page number in **bold type** a photograph. Both of these may be in addition to a text reference on the same page.

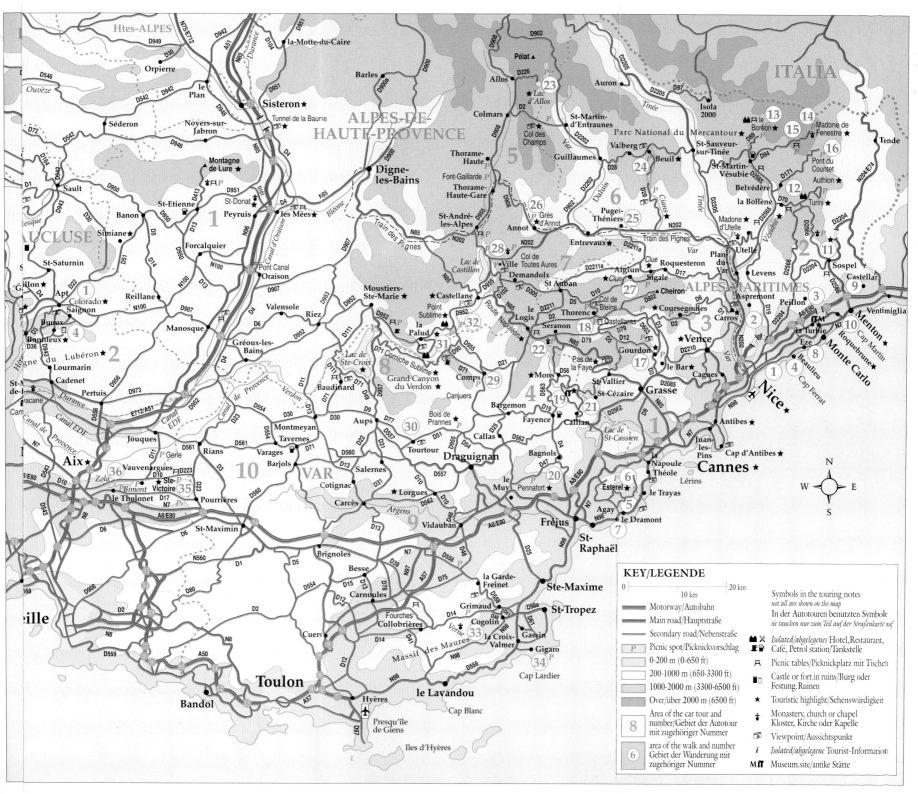

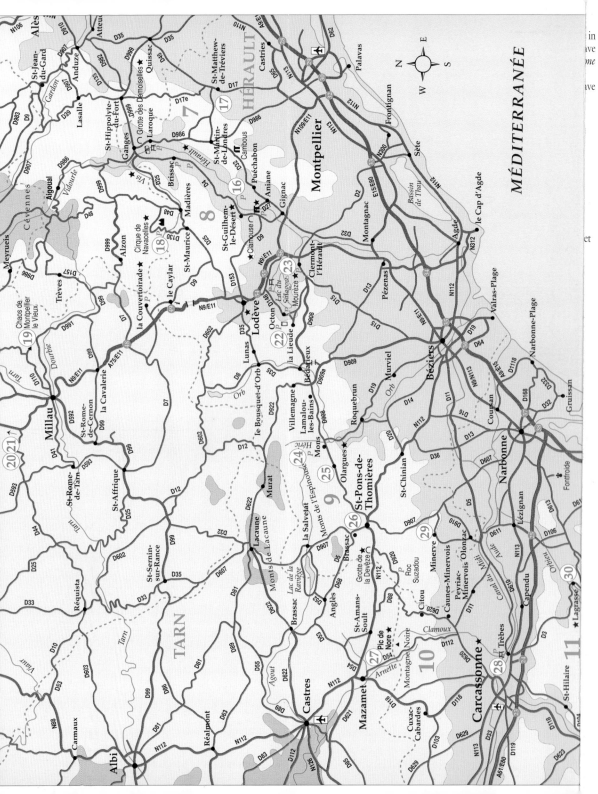